SHAKE, STIR, POUR

Quarry Books
100 Cummings Center, Suite 406L
Beverly, MA 01915

quarrybooks.com • craftside.typepad.com

First published in the United States of America in 2012 by
Quarry Books, a member of
Quayside Publishing Group
100 Cummings Center
Suite 406-L
Beverly, Massachusetts 01915-6101
Telephone: (978) 282-9590
Fax: (978) 283-2742
www.quarrybooks.com

10 9 8 7 6 5 4 3 2 1

ISBN: 978-1-59253-797-6

Digital edition published in 2012
eISBN: 978-1-61058-395-4

Library of Congress Cataloging-in-Publication Data available

Design: Rita Sowins / Sowins Design
Photography: Steve Legato, with the exception of page 137 from shutterstock.com

Printed in China

FOREWORD

Few chefs would deny the allure of a well-made cocktail at the end of a long shift, but the synergy between kitchen folk and bartenders extends well beyond our affinity for each other's craft. Today, as more and more budding mixologists expand their repertoire, they are developing techniques, flavors, and ingredients that chefs share.

Katie Loeb is one such mixologist. Beginning with her work behind the bar at Amada, my first restaurant, she showed a sensitivity to taste and a knack for bringing seemingly disparate flavors together into exceptional cocktails. At the heart of her work is her deep-seated respect for classic recipes and top-notch ingredients. But in an era when many trend-seeking would-be bartenders insist on slavishly following the old world cocktail groundwork laid out before Prohibition, Katie has sought to integrate those thoughtful recipes with her own passion for fresh herbs, rare spices, and seasonal fruit juices and purees. Through trial and error, she's developed a veritable library of juices, infusions, syrups, and other additives that elevate even the simplest cocktail recipe into an exciting new flavor experience.

As you page through *Shake, Stir, Pour*, I hope you will experiment with Katie's recipes, trying them out for yourself and serving them both as she suggests and in new and different ways that speak to you. Katie's willingness to break from tradition, to pour a different spirit into a cocktail or add an unusual flavor note to a well-loved recipe, is what makes her drinks special and that creative spirit can be found throughout the pages of this beautiful book. I encourage you to allow your palate to roam, as she does, adding unexpected touches to the drinks you and your friends know and love, and sharing them, as any well-made cocktail is meant to be shared.

Cheers.

Iron Chef Jose Garces

★ CONTENTS ★

INTRODUCTION ... 6

{ CHAPTER 1: TAKING STOCK } ... 8

Spirits ... 10
Bar Tools ... 17
Basic Glassware ... 20
Purchased Mixers/Garnishes ... 22
Kitchen Tools ... 24
Kitchen Staples ... 27

{ CHAPTER 2: SYRUPS } ... 32

Simple Syrup ... 34
Herbal Syrups ... 37
Spice Syrups ... 56
Fruit/Vegetable Syrups ... 70

{ CHAPTER 3: BAR BASICS } ... 92

Grenadine ... 94
Fresh Citrus Cordials ... 101
Ginger Beer ... 109
Cocktail Starters and Syrups ... 114
Cocktail Garnishes ... 122

{ CHAPTER 4: INFUSIONS } ... 128

Vodka/Gin Infusions ... 132
Infusions with a Kick ... 137
Limoncello ... 140
Aquavit ... 142
Tequila Por Mi Amante ... 144
Bitters ... 145

RESOURCE GUIDE ... 151
ABOUT THE AUTHOR ... 154
ABOUT THE PHOTOGRAPHER ... 154
ACKNOWLEDGMENTS ... 155
INDEX ... 156

{ DRINK LIST }

THAI BASIL SYRUP
Front Stoop Lemonade

MINT SYRUP
Mojito
Smoked Peach Bourbon Smash
Mint Julep

ROSEMARY SYRUP
Rosemary Lemonade
Rosemary Paloma

THYME SYRUP
Parisian Martini

LAVENDER SYRUP
Lavender Lemonade
Provençal Martini

HONEYSUCKLE SYRUP
The GMF
Canción de Flores

HIBISCUS SYRUP
Love in Bloom
Man-Full-O'-Trouble Punch

MIXED HERB SYRUP
Basic Herbal Cooler

DESSERT SPICED SYRUP
Mumbai Mule
Naughty Pilgrim
Basic Hot Toddy

CINNAMON SYRUP
Hot Apple Pie
Bark and Blood

CARDAMOM-KAFFIR LIME SYRUP
The Grape Gatsby

GINGERY SYRUP
Melon-choly Baby

ORANGE CARDAMOM SYRUP
Orange Cardamom Cooler

RHUBARB SYRUP
Rhuby Daiquiri

CELERY SYRUP
Jalisco Cel-Ray
Royster Cup

PEAR SYRUP
Pear Blossom

PEACH SYRUP
Better Bellini

BLUEBERRY SYRUP
Blueberry Lemonade

SMOKED PINEAPPLE SYRUP
Piña Doble

PASSION FRUIT SYRUP
Hurricane
Port Light

BLACKBERRY SHRUB

GRENADINE
Jack Rose
Scofflaw

**BLACK CURRANT-KAFFIR LIME
"GRENADINE"**
Purple Haze

**RUBY RED GRAPEFRUIT-
LEMONGRASS CORDIAL**
Hemingway Daiquiri

LEMON CORDIAL
Fresh Lemon Giblet

FRESH LIME CORDIAL
Salty Pomeranian
Fresh Lime Giblet

HOMEMADE GINGER BEER
Dark 'N' Stormy
Gin-Gin Mule
Pink Sapphire Swizzle

ORGEAT SYRUP
Mai Tai

FALERNUM
Rhum Ricardo

PIMENTO (OR ALLSPICE) DRAM
Lion's Tail
None But The Brave

TRUFFLE-HONEY SYRUP
Versailles

BASIC BLOODY MARY MIX
Smokin' Mary (or Smokin' Snapper
or Maria)

COCKTAIL ONIONS
Gibson

COCKTAIL CHERRIES
Money Manhattan

PINEAPPLE VODKA
Steakhouse Pineapple Martini

CUCUMBER VODKA/GIN
Cucumber Gimlet

**HORSERADISH VODKA (NEW
ENGLANDER)**

**CUCUMBER, LEMON & DILL GIN
(THE LONDONER)**
Bloody Mary Nichols

**SERAFIN (SERANO PEPPER AND
TARRAGON-INFUSED TEQUILA)**
Serafina Cocktail

**CHIHUAHUA (JALAPEÑO-
CILANTRO VODKA)**
Rabid Chihuahua

HOMEMADE LIMONCELLO

AQUAVIT
Bloody Viking
Rosalind Russell

TEQUILA POR MI AMANTE
Strawberry Margarita

SPICE BITTERS

COCK·TAIL *NOUN* \ˈKÄK-TĀL\

AN ICED DRINK OF WINE OR DISTILLED LIQUOR MIXED WITH FLAVORING INGREDIENTS

(Merriam-Webster's Collegiate Dictionary, 11th Edition)

With all due respect to the dictionary, this is the least inspired definition of a cocktail possible. I take great joy in the theatrics of cocktails and have great passion for creating them, and this dry and emotionless definition breaks my heart.

A cocktail can change your mood, delight you, inspire you. It is lovingly crafted and attractively presented. It can tease many senses before the glass is even raised to your lips. It is art, just like a delicious meal.

With the recent revival of cocktail culture, virtually every city has craft cocktail bars or finer dining establishments with a creative "signature" cocktail list. I've been fortunate enough to be a part of the cocktail movement in Philadelphia during this revival, both watching and tasting, and also playing along.

Over time, there has been a shift from bringing back the classics, to new creative twists on the classics, and then to making original concoctions with fresh, house-made ingredients. Just as the chef looks to the farmer for fresh, seasonal ingredients for his menu, bartenders are now sourcing their ingredients the same way. The "farm-to-bar" movement is thriving, and fresh syrups, mixers, produce, and juices have become the norm rather than the exception.

And I, for one, could not be more thrilled!

There are plenty of good reasons to make your own fresh cocktail ingredients.

BETTER FLAVOR. Once you've tasted the fresh version of a commercially bottled product, it's hard to ever go back.

STRAIGHT FROM THE SOURCE. Knowing the provenance of your ingredients is essential. No more artificial flavorings and colorings, chemicals, or high-fructose corn syrup. You are only drinking what you have chosen to pour into your glass.

PERSONAL CHOICE. Homemade cocktails mean you make whatever *you* like. Not a fan of lime? Make your gimlets from a lemon or grapefruit cordial. Have an abundance of berries from your garden or the local farmer's market? Preserve that fresh flavor in a shrub that will bring back a taste of summer on a frigid winter's night. Your creativity is limited only by what is available and what you have time to make.

SIMPLICITY. Making fresh cocktail ingredients is neither difficult nor all that time consuming.

It's forgiving too. It is not bomb making or birth control. Nothing earth shattering happens if you aren't scientifically precise. Follow the cocktail recipe the first time and then adjust it to your taste. If you want it sweeter or tarter, that's easy to shape. As you become more confident in building cocktails at home and in knowing your own tastes, you'll be able to adjust in advance.

»» Getting Your Feet (and Lips) Wet ««

I would love to pretend that my colleagues and I are formidable geniuses behind the bar, but the truth is, almost anyone who can shop, boil water, measure ingredients, and operate basic kitchen equipment can craft homegrown cocktails. There are a few basic techniques to be mastered and, after that, you're off and running.

The finest bartenders in the world know their customers, what a customer wants before he or she knows, how to gently educate without being overbearing or unpleasant, how to enhance a guest's experience, and how to prepare a cocktail with flourish. Home cocktail aficionados only need to please and entertain themselves, their friends, guests, and family. And while the best mixologists are one part creative chef, one part intuitive waiter, and one part "spiritual advisor," you do not need to possess a professional bartender's entire skill set to prepare fresh bar ingredients at home. That's one of the easiest parts of the job!

»» This Book Is for You. Trust Me. ««

If you are an accomplished home chef who enjoys entertaining, I hope you come away from reading this book with new ideas for impressing your guests. Even if you aren't a seasoned cook, there are plenty of simple techniques and recipes that virtually anyone can make. If you don't drink alcohol, there are plenty of nonalcoholic uses for these recipes. *Shake, Stir, Pour— Fresh Homegrown Cocktails* is simply for anyone who wants to recreate the delicious cocktails at their favorite restaurant or bar at home.

I hope this book demystifies the process, and builds your confidence in the kitchen so you can taste (pun intended) the joy and energy that I get from creating cocktails.

So, what is my proposed definition of a cocktail?

A DRINK CRAFTED WITH LOVE, FASHIONED FROM THE FINEST SPIRITS, AND ENHANCED WITH FRESH INGREDIENTS, THAT DELIGHTS YOUR SENSES, PLEASES YOUR PALATE, AND LEAVES YOU HAPPIER THAN YOU WERE BEFORE YOU POURED IT.

That's a cocktail!
CHEERS!

CHAPTER 1

TAKING STOCK

If you already entertain guests by mixing basic cocktails and/or cooking for your family, you may have most everything you need. It isn't necessary to spend a fortune or have tons of storage space for fancy spirits, expensive glasses, and specialty tools. All you need to begin is a basic, minimally stocked bar, bar tools, and some familiar kitchen items that you may already own. Knowing what to shop for, where to find it, and how to choose your ingredients wisely is your next step.

In this chapter you will learn how to stock a basic, versatile home bar with:

★ Spirits and liqueurs
★ Bar tools, kitchen tools, and glassware
★ Mixers and garnishes (to purchase)
★ Cookware and small appliances
★ Pantry staples, such as sweeteners, spices, fresh fruit, produce, herbs, and more
★ The best products from local farmers' markets and ethnic markets

It isn't necessary to have the enormous selection of your favorite restaurant bar since it isn't likely you'll have to please the whims of a hundred guests. If you have a favorite brand of any kind of spirit, by all means stock your bar with it. In my experience as a bartender, many people tend to order the same thing out of habit, not always preference. That said, a little experimentation at a well-stocked bar to try some new brands in your favorite drink is always a good idea. You might surprise yourself and discover a new brand.

....

**To sample new flavors or brands, try buying "mini" bottles at the liquor store.
It's a low-commitment way to try something new.**

....

If you have expensive tastes, I recommend buying premium spirits for sipping straight or with the least number of other mixers. There's little sense in spending a lot of money on spirits only to mask their subtle nuances with a lot of other flavors. However, inexpensive spirits should be avoided, since they are not made with the same level of care, and higher levels of unpleasant hangover-inducing impurities may be present. The old adage "you get what you pay for" rings true with spirits.

⋆ SPIRITS ⋆

A basic selection of one or two of each of the following spirits should be adequate for almost any home bar and allow you to mix up a cocktail from this book for virtually any taste.

»» Vodka ««

Vodka is distilled primarily from grain or potatoes, although it can be made from almost any fermentable carbohydrate including rice, apples, grapes, or other fruits. It has been produced in Russia since approximately the late ninth century. It is also popular in Poland and other Eastern European countries. Vodka's appeal is that it is virtually flavorless, and hence blends pleasantly with all other flavors. For cocktails that are primarily comprised of vodka, such as a martini, a premium brand such as Grey Goose, Chopin, or Belvedere might be preferable. However, for most infusions or cocktails containing juices and freshly made syrups, a more economical choice is wiser. Smirnoff is widely available and perfectly suited for any of the recipes in this book. Eighty proof (or 40% alcohol by volume) vodka is called for in most cocktail recipes. I recommend having overproof, or 100 proof, vodka for certain infusions and for use as a preservative in freshly made syrups. A small amount of 100 proof vodka gives syrups a great deal more shelf stability once refrigerated. Flavored vodkas can make variations of your favorite cocktails easy to achieve and will expand your repertoire of cocktails for entertaining.

»» Gin ««

The Dutch word *jenever* means "juniper," and gin is a spirit distilled with a predominant flavor of juniper berries. Like many spirits, gin was originally a medicinal spirit, and juniper was thought to have curative powers for ailments as wide ranging as kidney problems, lumbago, stomach ailments, gallstones, and gout. It was being produced by hundreds of Dutch and Belgian distillers by the mid-seventeenth century by redistillation of malt spirit or wine with juniper, anise, caraway, coriander, and other spices. English troops fighting against the Spanish in the Eighty Years' War in Holland discovered its calming effects before battle and coined the term "Dutch courage." When William of Orange ascended to the English throne in 1689, gin's popularity in England was secured for the foreseeable future.

London dry gin is the style most common today, made by redistilling neutral grain spirits with juniper and citrus botanicals, such as lemon, bitter (Seville) orange, lime or grapefruit peel, as well as a combination of other spices, possibly including anise, angelica root and seed, orris (iris) root, licorice root, cinnamon, almond, cubeb, savory, saffron, coriander, grains of paradise, nutmeg, and cassia bark. London dry gin may not contain added sugar or colorants; water is the only permitted additive. Some examples of this style include Tanqueray, Beefeater, Bombay, and Gordon's.

Plymouth gin is a smooth full-bodied gin that originated in the port of Plymouth on the English Channel. It has a distinctively different, slightly less dry flavor than London dry gin.

"New generation" gins have become more popular in the last decade or so, and are meant to appeal to the drinker who doesn't fancy the big Christmas-tree flavor of juniper in a London dry-style gin. These gins bring the other botanicals to the forefront and dial back the juniper in the flavor profile. Some examples of this style include Bluecoat, distilled in Philadelphia, which is more citrus forward, and Hendricks, which is produced in Scotland and includes the subtle flavor of cucumber and rose petals.

»» Rum ««

Rum is a spirit distilled from sugar cane; either directly from fermented sugar cane juice as is *rhum agricole* in Martinique or Cachaça in Brazil, or from fermented molasses as it is in most of the Caribbean and Central America. The resulting clear distillate is then aged in barrels to give it smoothness and color, or stainless steel tanks so it remains colorless. Once the rum is aged it is then generally blended. In some cases this requires the filtering of the rum to remove color so the rum can be bottled as a "silver" or "white" rum. These lighter rums are generally used for cocktails. Sometimes caramel is added to the rum during the blending process for color and flavor. The resulting golden or amber rums have more flavor than their white counterparts and can be mixed into cocktails or consumed straight over ice. Significantly aged *añejo* rums are generally made for sipping with little or no ice. Dark rums are generally aged in charred oak barrels that give them a very dark color and heavy body. They are often used in combination with lighter rums in tiki-style cocktails.

Overproof rums, such as Bacardi 151 or Wray and Nephew white overproof rum at 124 proof (62% alcohol by volume), are often used in tiki-style drinks or as the base for homemade spirits such as pimento dram or falernum.

»» Tequila and Mescal ««

(Note: Tequila regulatory information courtesy of tequila.net)
Tequila is a spirit distilled from the heart of the blue agave cactus, restricted to the area surrounding the town of Tequila in the western region of Jalisco, Mexico. The Aztecs had long enjoyed a milky fermented cactus beer known as *pulque*, but the Spanish conquistadors were the first to distill what we now know as tequila, the national drink of Mexico.

Tequila is still produced in much the same way that it has been for centuries, unchanged by modern farming technologies. The agave plants are tended and raised by *jimadores*, who possess generations of knowledge about the plants and the methods of hand harvesting. The jimadores must pick the plants at the precise age at which the sugars are at peak ripeness, and then manually cut away the outer leaves using a special bladed tool, revealing the inner *piña*, a 40–80 pound core so named for its resemblance to a pineapple. The *piña* are roasted in giant ovens to concentrate the sugars and then shredded and pressed to extract the juices. The juice is then allowed to ferment in either wood or stainless steel vats for several days to ferment the sugars into alcohol. The yeasts used by each manufacturer are a closely guarded secret. The fermented product is then distilled once to produce a milky liquid, and then distilled a second time to produce a clear, silver tequila which is then diluted and bottled as a "silver tequila," or it is

When purchasing tequila, it's important to seek out those which are made with 100% agave, as indicated clearly on the neck of this product.

pumped into barrels to begin the aging process. Some producers distill a third time, but many tequila aficionados feel that this step removes too many subtle flavors from the finished product.

There are two basic categories of tequila: mixtos and 100% agave. Mixtos use a minimum of 51% agave, with other sugars making up the remainder. These products tend to be less expensive and often contain artificial colorings. I recommend always seeking out 100% agave tequila, which will be clearly labeled as such. As with other cask-aged spirits, barrel aging will mellow the tequila, removing the harsh flavors and adding flavor components from the wood, such as vanillins.

Tequila is usually bottled in one of five categories:

★ Blanco ("white") or plata ("silver"): white spirit, unaged and bottled or aged less than two months in stainless steel or neutral oak barrels;
★ Joven ("young") or oro ("gold"): a mixture of blanco tequila and reposado tequila (Ex. José Cuervo Oro);
★ Reposado ("rested"): aged a minimum of two months, but less than twelve months in oak barrels of any size;
★ Añejo ("aged" or "vintage"): aged a minimum of one year, but less than three years in small oak barrels;
★ Extra Añejo ("extra aged" or "ultra-aged"): aged a minimum of three years in oak barrels.

Some of the widely available brands of premium tequilas include Sauza, Herradura, Espolon, Siembra Azul, Corralejo, and Partida.

Tequila mixes well with citrus flavors as in a classic Margarita or Paloma, but also works really well with fruity/berry flavors like cassis, strawberry, or raspberry.

Although not as well known as tequila, mescal is another native spirit that is produced in the Oaxaca region of Mexico. While tequila is produced exclusively from the blue agave plant, mescal can be produced from any of several species of *maguey* (maguey is another name for agave) plants. In much the same way that all cognac is brandy, but not all brandy is cognac, one could say that tequila is a variety of mescal, but not all mescal is tequila. The primary differences between the two spirits is both in the species of plants from which it is distilled and the production method.

Its distinctive roasting and distillation process is what gives mescal its intense and unique smoky flavor. The piñas are cooked in underground ovens for days, trapping the smoke inside and imparting that flavor to the finished product.

Mescal is generally distilled only once, rather than at least twice like tequila, and the resulting spirit is much less smooth as a result. Mescal is generally drunk straight, in a shot, or sipped. There is no "signature cocktail" like the margarita made from mescal, so it is far less widely known and appreciated. Mescal added to a cocktail in small amounts can add a subtle smokiness and delicious dimension of flavor and aroma. Higher end single-village mescals such as those produced by Del Maguey are as unique and delicious as single-village Burgundies, and are well worth exploring if you find you enjoy the distinctive flavor of mescal.

»» Bourbon ««

Bourbon is a barrel-aged distilled spirit made primarily from corn. Bourbon is so named due to its strong association with what is now known as Bourbon County, Kentucky. Bourbon County was originally a part of the Commonwealth of Virginia, an enormous expanse of land encompassing a large part of what is now northeastern Kentucky. This entire tract was known as "Old Bourbon," in honor of the French royal family of the same name. Since the late eighteenth century, Scottish, Irish, English, German, and Welsh immigrants farmed those lands. Being resourceful peoples, they began to distill the local corn into whiskey. In the early nineteenth century, distribution of whiskey occurred via shipping down the Ohio River, and the barrels of corn whiskey from this region began to be stamped "Old Bourbon" to show their place of origin and to distinguish them from the primarily rye-based whiskeys that were being produced in western Pennsylvania and were often shipped on the same boats. Eventually, bourbon became the name for any sort of corn whiskey.

To legally qualify as bourbon, the spirit must be made from a grain mixture that is at least 51 percent corn, the remainder of this grain mixture, or *mash bill*, being wheat and/or rye, and malted barley. Bourbon must be aged in new, charred oak barrels and must be distilled to no more than 160 proof (80% alcohol by volume). Like other whiskeys, bourbon must be bottled at 80 proof or more (40% alcohol by volume). It must enter the barrel for aging at no higher than 125 proof (62.5% alcohol by volume). And while there is no minimum specified duration for its aging period, it must be aged at least briefly.

Unaged corn whiskey, more commonly referred to as "moonshine," is making a comeback in the market. It has a sweet flavor and aromas reminiscent of marshmallows and cotton candy, but generally lacks the smoothness that the barrel-aging imparts.

Bourbon is a sweeter spirit that mixes well with other sweet flavors or mint, as in the classic Manhattan or Mint Julep cocktail.

»» Scotch Whiskey ««

Scotch whiskey is produced in Scotland. It must be made from water, malted barley, and yeast, to which other whole grains such as wheat and/or corn may be added. It must be aged for a minimum of three years in oak casks to a minimum strength of 80 proof (40% alcohol by volume). "Malting" the barley grains is actually a controlled germination process, where the grains are allowed to begin to sprout, releasing enzymes that begin to break down starches in the grain and convert them to sugars. The distinctive tangy smokiness of many scotches comes from drying the malted barley over fires stoked with peat, a form of compacted grass and heather compost that burns slowly and gives off aromatic smoke as it smolders.

There are fewer classic cocktails made with Scotch, although the Rob Roy (a Scotch Manhattan) and the Blood and Sand (made with Scotch whiskey, cherry brandy, sweet vermouth, and orange juice) are well known.

Scotch begins as either:
★ Single-malt Scotch, which is produced at a single distillery in a pot still and contains only malted barley, water, and yeast.
★ Single-grain Scotch whiskey, which is produced at a single distillery in either a pot or a column still but contains other cereal grains in addition to the malted barley. The word *single* refers to one distillery, not the use of a single type of grain.

It is from these two main types of Scotch whiskey that all blended Scotch is created.

★ Blended malt whisky is a blend of two or more single-malt Scotch whiskeys from different distilleries.
★ Blended grain whiskey is a blend of two or more single-grain Scotch whiskeys from different distilleries.
★ Blended Scotch whiskey means a blend of one or more single-malt Scotch whiskeys with one or more single-grain Scotch whiskeys.

There are four main regions that produce Scotch whiskey, and each has a distinctive style. **The Highlands** covers all of the area north of Dundee on the North Sea coast in the east to Greenock on the Irish Sea in the west and includes all of the islands off of the mainland with the exception of Islay. Highland Scotch whiskey is generally medium-bodied, smooth, and aromatic and range from delicate and floral to lush and complex.

The Lowlands encompasses all of the Scottish mainland south of the Highlands with the exception of the Campbeltown Peninsula. Lowland Scotches tend to be lighter bodied, sweeter, and more delicate.

Campbeltown is a port located on the tip of the Kintyre Peninsula on the southwest coast. These Scotches have their own distinctive spicy and salt-tinged flavor.

Islay is an island off the west coast of the mainland. Traditional Islay malt whiskeys are intensely smoky and pungent and have a very distinctive iodine or "kelpy" tang that is said to come from sea salt permeating the local peat that is used to dry the barley malt.

»» Cognac ««

Cognac is a specific type of brandy that is named for the city in France around which it is produced. This wine-producing region extends along the banks of the Charente River all the way to the Atlantic coast of western France. Cognac has a long and storied history. The vineyards of Cognac have existed since as far back as the Gallo-Roman times and were probably planted during the last part of the third century CE. by the Romans.

Cognac is a heavily regulated spirit, and there are certain rigorous processes that must be followed regarding its production and aging before it is available for consumption. Cognac must be made from certain grapes (primarily ugni blanc) and must be distilled twice in copper alembic pot stills. No additives are permitted and the minimum alcohol content must be 40% alcohol by volume. Cognac must be aged for a minimum of two years in Limousin or Tronçais French oak barrels. Most cognacs are aged considerably longer than the minimum legal requirement.

Cognac is the base for the classic Sidecar cocktail. Cognac mixes well with citrus, autumn fruits like apple and pear, and floral flavors.

»» Aperitifs and Specialty Liqueurs ««

Vermouth is an aromatized wine that is flavored with various dry ingredients including cloves, cinnamon, quinine, citrus peel, cardamom, marjoram, chamomile, coriander, juniper, hyssop, ginger, and wormwood. In fact, the word "vermouth" is a corruption of the German *wermut*, or wormwood, also an ingredient in absinthe that has been used in the drink over its history. Vermouth was originally used for medicinal purposes, but eventually became a popular ingredient for classic cocktails. Two distinct styles emerged, the clear, dry, and bitter "French" style and the red, sweeter "Italian" style, although both types are produced in each country.

There are several producers that make exceptional vermouths, worthy of drinking on their own as an aperitif on the rocks, or for really making a cocktail special. Chambéry, France, is the only region that has earned an Appellation d'Origine for their vermouths.

Carpano is Italy's finest vermouth producer and the Antica Formula is barrel-aged and adds a rich flavor and complexity to any cocktail.

Maraschino is so named for the Croatian Marasca cherries from which it is distilled. Cherries are crushed with their pits still intact, which lend an almondlike note and indescribable unique flavor to this liqueur. This is an ingredient used in small doses, as its unique flavor can be quite overwhelming, but it is an essential ingredient in many classic cocktails like the Martinez and the Last Word.

Triple Sec/Orange Curaçao is an orange-flavored liqueur made from the dried peels of bitter and sweet oranges. It is utilized as the sweetener in many classic cocktails such as a Margarita or a Sidecar. Cointreau or Luxardo Triplum are both high quality brands and can be used interchangeably in these recipes.

Benedictine is an aromatic Cognac-based herbal liqueur originally produced by Benedictine monks at the Abbey de Fecamp in Normandy, France. It has a slightly sweet and very aromatic herbal flavor. It can be used to add sweetness and dimension to cocktails.

Chartreuse, like Benedictine is an herbal liqueur produced by monks, in this case the Carthusian Order of La Grande Chartreuse based near Grenoble, France. The formulation of 130 herbs, plants, and botanicals began as an "elixir of long life" on an alchemist's manuscript in 1605, and was passed down through the order. The modern recipe for what we now know as Chartreuse has remained the same since it was perfected in 1764: 110 proof, brilliant green, and powerfully aromatic. The color comes from chlorophyll in the plants used to produce it. The flavor is decidedly sweet, a little spicy, and very pungent. A sweeter, lower proof (80, or 40% alcohol by volume) yellow Chartreuse was developed in 1838. It is sweetened with honey and colored with saffron.

Green Chartreuse is used in several classic cocktails such as the Last Word and the Bijou. It is generally used sparingly, as its flavor and high proof level can easily overwhelm the other ingredients. Yellow Chartreuse works well as a sweetening agent in cocktails, and adds a layer of depth and herbaceous flavors that no other ingredient can quite reproduce.

★ BAR TOOLS ★

All the tools you need for making homegrown cocktails are available at either a kitchen supply retailer, the housewares area of your favorite department store, or a restaurant supply store (at wholesale prices).

Here's what you'll need:

★ **A SHAKER.** I suggest either a Boston Shaker, which consists of two halves—either one glass and one metal, or one large and one small metal half—and a Hawthorne strainer which has a large spring around it that fits into either half; or a three-part "cobbler" shaker that consists of a larger bottom portion and a top portion with a built-in strainer and a cap.

★ **A LONG-HANDLED BAR SPOON** for stirring drinks and occasionally measuring small amounts of ingredients. Try to find one with a spiral handle so you can twist it between your fingers while stirring, making mixing far more efficient.

★ **A SET OF JIGGERS** for measuring for consistent results. Look for a small 2-ounce (60 ml) metal measure with the measurements slanted inside the cup for ease of reading. The standard two-sided jiggers come with various combinations of measures on each side. If you have a large jigger that measures 2 ounces and 1 ounce (60 ml and 28 ml) and a small one that measures ½ ounce and ¼ ounce (14 ml and 7 ml) you will be prepared for any eventuality.

★ **A SMALL MESH STRAINER** for straining cocktails that might have particulate matter not captured in the first straining that would be aesthetically and texturally displeasing in your glass.

★ **A SMALL CUTTING BOARD** and **PARING KNIFE** that are dedicated to the bar for cutting fruit garnishes.

★ A good-quality **VEGETABLE PEELER** for cutting fresh citrus "twists" for garnish. Always cut citrus twists immediately before use so they do not dry out and so there is ample citrus oil in the zest to spray on the drink and flavor it. I like the "Y"-shaped peelers; look for a sharp swivel blade and a comfortable handle.

★ **A CHANNEL KNIFE** for cutting thin strips of citrus zest for garnish. These strips are more uniform and pretty, so they are best for decorative twists (and not as a strip of zest for flavoring a drink).

★ **CITRUS ZESTER** for removing tiny strips of zest for garnishes or cooking.

★ **A CITRUS PRESS** or "Mexican elbow" for fresh-squeezed lemon/lime juice.

★ An electric or manual press **JUICER** for larger fruits such as oranges and grapefruits as well as lemons and limes. (Centrifugal juicers that can be used to juice whole fruits and vegetables are mentioned later in the chapter.)

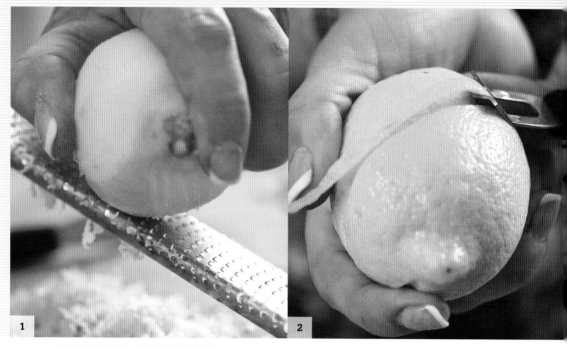

TOOLS FOR ZESTING AND JUICING CITRUS

1. A microplane zester finely grates citrus peel into its most fragrant form. **2.** A channel knife cuts beautiful, even strips of citrus peel for picture-perfect decorative twists. **3.** You can curl your twists by wrapping them tight like a spring around a wooden chopstick or dowel before garnishing your glass. **4.** Little strips of zest on the surface of a drink add aromatics that smell delicious as you lift the glass to your lips.

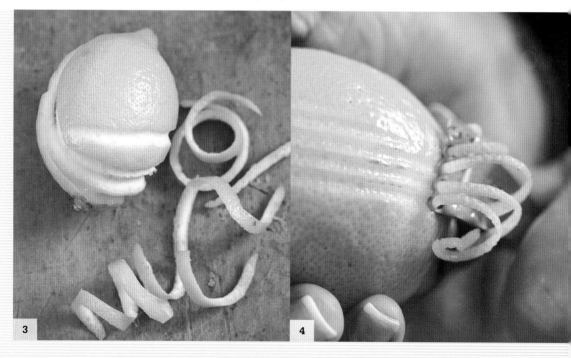

1

BAR TOOLS

1. A bar spoon is useful for stirring finished drinks. **2.** A blender helps puree and combine your drink ingredients. **3.** Jiggers come in many different styles. A double-sided handled one such as this is easy to use. Make certain the measurements are easy for you to utilize. A 1 once/2 ounce (30 ml/60 ml) size is most versatile.

2

3

★ BASIC GLASSWARE ★

I *love* cocktail glasses and vintage barware. I collect them, regardless of the space considerations of my cabinets. The older vintage glasses are just so lovely, and magically everything tastes better in a beautiful glass. I find an abundance of glasses, tools, and shakers at thrift stores, at yard and garage sales, and online. Combing the thrift stores and consignment shops in wealthier neighborhoods can uncover all manner of treasures. Sometimes it isn't just the monetary value of what you've found, but the thrill of the hunt and the satisfaction of finding that gorgeous set of etched or stemmed glasses that you know will be the perfect accoutrement for setting the lovely table you've envisioned for your guests. Many of the drinks photographed in this book are in glassware from my personal collection. However, you don't need fancy glassware to entertain or enjoy your own cocktail creations. A few basic glasses should cover virtually any circumstance.

★ **OLD-FASHIONED OR "ROCKS"** glasses are short and round and typically 8–10 ounces (240–300 ml) in volume. They are used for cocktails or liquor served on ice or with a "splash."

★ **HIGHBALL** glasses are tall and straight sided and 8–12 ounces (240 to 360 ml) in volume. Used for "tall" cocktails and mixer-combined liquor drinks (i.e. gin and tonic). A collins glass is a slightly taller highball glass around 14 ounces (415 ml). They can be used interchangeably.

★ **COCKTAIL/MARTINI/"BIRDBATH"** glasses have triangular shaped bowls on long footed stems. These glasses are used for a wide array of cocktails served straight up (without ice), including martinis, manhattans, and gimlets. These range in size from the older smaller 4–6 ounces (150 to 180 ml) glasses to the much larger 7–12 ounces (210 to 360 ml) glasses more popular today. I prefer the smaller glasses because the drink stays colder from beginning to end and I can have more of them without getting too inebriated.

»» Optional ««

★ **COUPE** or Saucer glasses are shallow, broad-bowled, stemmed glasses, commonly used for champagne. These are typically 5–6 ounces (150 to 180 ml) in size. Coupes are used for cocktails as an alternative to the V-shaped cocktail glass and in particular for daiquiris, margaritas, and other fruity drinks.

★ **CHAMPAGNE FLUTE** glasses are tall, narrow glasses with a small opening on a long stem, resembling a stretched-out wine glass. The stem allows the drinker to hold the glass without raising the temperature of the chilled champagne, and the narrow opening at the top reduces the surface area so the carbonation is retained for a longer period of time. These glasses are used for serving champagne or sparkling wine and cocktails that are based on those ingredients.

★ **BRANDY SNIFTERS** are bulbous glasses with a smaller opening on a short stem. The shape of this glass concentrates the alcoholic aromas to the top of the glass as your hands warm the spirit. This glass is typically used for brandy, cognac, armagnac, or aged spirits for sipping. These vary in size from 4–20 ounces (120 to 600 ml) so there's a large range. These glasses make a nice presentation for cognac- or brandy-based cocktails such as a Sidecar or as an alternative to the more usual cocktail or coupe glasses for straight-up drinks with room for lots of garnish.

1. Rocks glasses are used for cocktails or liquor served on ice or with a "splash." **2.** Collins and highball glasses are used for "tall" drinks or mixers. **3.** Cocktail/"martini" and coupe glasses for cocktails served "up." **4.** Champagne flutes allow you to hold the glass without raising the temperature of the chilled champagne. **5.** Snifters are for Cognac and brandy-based drinks.

CREATIVE SERVING OPTIONS

Sometimes, an unusual choice for a serving vessel can really make a statement.

★ Punches or spiked ice tea or lemonades look great in mason jars.
★ Using mugs or fancy tea cups, even mismatched ones, are a practical and attractive way to serve hot toddies or mulled wine.
★ Jelly jars or canning jars are a neat way to serve wine or juice-based cocktails.

That picture-perfect Victorian "tablescape" straight out of an Edith Wharton novel is a lovely goal to aspire to, but few of us live under such rigid and formal circumstances or own all of the accessories to achieve that, even if we wanted to. Just as there are no rules telling you what to put in your glass, there are no rules governing what constitutes a glass. It's all up to you. Have fun with it and don't worry about setting a "proper" table.

★ PURCHASED MIXERS/GARNISHES ★

While this book will teach you to make your own mixers and flavoring syrups from scratch, there will always be a need to keep a supply of purchased basic mixers around the house. Many of these are probably in your refrigerator or cupboard already.

»» Sodas ««

Cola (regular or diet, depending on your preference), ginger ale, lemon-lime soda, club soda, tonic water, bitter lemon (a citrus flavored tonic) are your basics. I'm fond of some of the newer premium mixers like the Fever-Tree line and Q Tonic. These can often be found at specialty stores or through online retailers.

»» Juices ««

Orange juice, cranberry juice, pineapple juice, and grapefruit juice are those most commonly called for. Buy juices that are not from concentrate whenever possible. Lemon or lime juice is generally called for in small enough amounts so that juicing fresh fruit can be done as needed.

For larger amounts of juice, such as for making cordials or batches of drinks for a party, I recommend finding fresh-squeezed, fresh-frozen, or minimally pasteurized fresh juices.

One company that is widely distributed is Natalie's Orchid Island Juice Company. This company's products are always fresh tasting and are kosher certified as well. Never use the commercially manufactured lemon or lime juices in the fruit-shaped bottles. Juices from fruit concentrates do not contain the whole fruits, and they may be nothing much more than sugar water. In addition, juices made from imported produce may carry traces of banned pesticides. Stick with fresh-squeezed juices, by either your own hand or a reputable fresh juice provider.

Smaller 10-ounce (300 ml) soda bottles or 5.5-ounce (165 ml) juice cans in the six-packs are very handy if you don't want to be wasteful. One small bottle/can has enough in it to make several cocktails, and if you only end up making one drink you only waste a little bit of mixer, not a big two-liter bottle of it. Another neat trick is to store your opened and tightly recapped carbonated beverages upside down. If the air pocket is at the end of the bottle where it has no escape the contents won't go flat nearly as quickly. It looks a little strange on the shelves or in the refrigerator door, but it works like a charm.

»» Cocktail Cherries ««

I hesitate to use the word "maraschino" cherries because what most people think of as cocktail cherries are the worst sort of pollutant to place into a lovingly crafted cocktail.

The modern bleached, artificially dyed and sweetened maraschino cherry is actually a result of Prohibition. During Prohibition, Croatian Marasca cherries preserved in Maraschino liqueur (true maraschino cherries) were illegal due to their alcohol content. The process of bleaching

Queen Anne cherries in brine and then artificially coloring and sweetening them was developed as a replacement for the no-longer-legal imported delicacy.

If you need cherries for your Manhattans or other cocktails, use real organic cherries preserved in liquor or syrup, such as Luxardo Gourmet Cherries, Amarena Fabbri, or Les Parissiennes. You can also easily make them yourself, and I have included a recipe in this book (see page 124).

»» Cocktail Onions ««

Most bottled cocktail onions are essentially flavorless small pearl onions in brine. Sable & Rosenfeld "tipsy" onions or Silver Palate cocktail onions are a couple of commercial brands that use vermouth as a preservative, and these are a vastly superior alternative. Cocktail onions are also easy to make at home. A recipe is included in this book (see page 122).

OPTIONAL KITCHEN EQUIPMENT THAT MIGHT BE VERY HANDY

»» Juicers ««

★ **A MANUAL JUICER:** Consists of a stand with a base, reamer cup, and extractor arm that exerts enough pressure to fully extract all of the juice from a halved citrus fruit. These come apart for easy cleaning.

★ **AN ELECTRIC CITRUS JUICER** is essentially a motorized reamer that fits citrus fruits of all sizes and allows you to press down the flesh of the fruit onto the moving reamer portion and drain off the juice to either a separate compartment or separate container through a spout.

★ **A POWER JUICER** is a heavy-duty juice extractor that can handle all sorts of fruits and vegetables, both hard and soft. Generally it has a high speed motor, some form of mesh filter, a pulp collection area for the solid matter, and a juice collection container.

★ **A SODA SIPHON OR CARBONATION MACHINE** is good for creating your own carbonated beverages from your flavored syrups or carbonating water for house-made seltzer/club soda. Models may vary but some soda siphons are powered by small nitrous oxide cartridges. Carbonation machines are available at department stores and are powered by proprietary CO_2 cartridges.

★ KITCHEN TOOLS ★

Most of what you need is likely in your kitchen already if you cook at all. This is a short checklist of items you'll need to create your own syrups, mixers, and garnishes.

»» Cookware/Appliances ««

★ **A SMALL SAUCEPAN** with a lid (2–3 quart [or about 2l to 3l ml] capacity) for small batches of simple syrup.

★ **A BASIC MEDIUM SAUCEPAN** with a lid. The 6-quart size (or 5.5 liter) is a good size and will handle almost any recipe requirements. A nonstick surface is easier to clean, particularly since many of these recipes are for sticky, syrupy-textured liquids.

A professional fine mesh chinoise is an irreplaceable kitchen tool for straining out small bits of natural (but unpalatable) ingredients in syrups (as well as soups and stocks).

★ **A LARGE COLANDER** for straining fruits or vegetables after blanching.

★ **A LARGE FINE-MESH STRAINER** for removing cellulose, seeds, and other fibrous materials from finished syrups, juices, and cordials. A professional *chinoise*, or conical extra-fine-mesh sieve can be an excellent investment for large batches. It is used in commercial kitchens to strain custards, purees, soups, and sauces, producing a very smooth texture. A small gold mesh coffee filter is also useful for smaller jobs.

★ **A COMMERCIAL-GRADE BLENDER**, your most-used item for making syrups, purees, and fresh juices; something equipped with a powerful motor of a minimum of 2 horsepower and with stainless steel blades for effective blending. Waring, Vitamix, Blendtec, and HealthMaster all make models that fit this criteria. Sometimes the word "commercial" or "professional" will be in the model name. While a regular consumer blender can handle most of the tasks required, it isn't meant to take the sort of repetitive use that the commercial brands are, and it could break down or overheat if you use them too frequently. It also doesn't have the motor power to crush hard seeds and spices without damage to the unit. It is better to invest in a really good blender just once and know that it is the proper tool for the job. It is possible to find these blenders at deep discounts online, or at restaurant equipment auctions. Amazon.com and eBay are good resources for this.

★ A good **SET OF MEASURING DEVICES** is crucial. The angled measuring cups from OXO are easy to read from above without having to stop and check for adjustments, are dishwasher and microwave safe, and have both standard and metric markings. If you're short on space, a 2-cup (475 ml) and a 4-cup (946 ml) measure should cover virtually any circumstance. Jiggers from the bar can handle smaller liquid volume measurements in a pinch.

★ **MEASURING SPOONS.** Stainless steel spoons are easier to clean and can take a beating. Shape isn't important, although I personally find the rectangular spoons easier to fill and read.

★ **VEGETABLE PEELER.** A second peeler for the kitchen cabinet will keep you from running to the bar every time you need to use this. The small "eyer" loop on one side of the blade is for removing blemishes on fruit or vegetables and is quite useful.

★ **A MICROPLANE** for removing only the zest from citrus fruits, without any of the bitter pith. Microplaning exposes more surface area of the zest for better infusions and more flavorful syrups.

★ **LARGE WOODEN OR SILICONE SPOON** for stirring while cooking.

★ **LADLE** for pressing down on solids while straining and transferring finished syrups to storage containers.

★ **A POTATO MASHER** for mashing fruits or pressing on solids while straining.

★ **A LARGE POLYPROPYLENE CUTTING BOARD** for preparing fruits, vegetables, and herbs. These are dishwasher safe and easy to clean.

★ A sharp **PARING KNIFE** for skinning fruits and vegetables.

★ **A MEDIUM COOK'S KNIFE** for chopping herbs and slicing.

★ **A WHISK** for whisking and breaking up fibers in fruit purees and syrups.

★ **AN APPLE DIVIDER** for coring and slicing apples and pears.

★ **A CHERRY/OLIVE PITTER** for removing seeds and pits prior to cooking, serving, or preserving.

★ **A SALAD SPINNER** for drying fresh herbs after rinsing.

★ **A COFFEE GRINDER** for chopping/grinding hard spices.

★ **A ROLLING PIN** for bruising herbs and crushing spices. A small bottle can substitute in a pinch.

★ A stovetop/grill-top **SMOKER** for smoking vegetables and fruits. I have a small NordicWare stovetop smoker that has a nonstick smoker pan and is easy to use and clean.

1. A well-made measuring cup with easy-to-read markings can be your best friend in the kitchen. **2.** Your measuring spoons will get a workout. Make sure they're good quality and easy to read and clean. **3.** A potato masher helps to press the last bits of liquid out when straining solids from your creations. **4.** A cherry or olive pitter removes seeds/pits prior to cooking or preserving. **5.** A small stove/grill-top smoker is a great kitchen accessory either for smoking cocktail ingredients or for smoking your main dish.

★ KITCHEN STAPLES ★

The staples you need for creating syrups and mixers are likely to be in your kitchen already. You just might need to start purchasing them in larger quantities than you did for only occasional use.

»» Sugar and Other Sweeteners ««

★ **GRANULATED WHITE CANE SUGAR** is the common everyday sugar that is in almost everyone's cupboard. It is readily available and can be found in almost any supermarket or convenience store. It has been processed to remove any traces of coloring from molasses. Organic, unbleached varieties can often be found at specialty food stores and health food stores. These may have trace amounts of molasses in them, but are interchangeable with the supermarket variety of granulated white sugar.

★ **DEMERARA SUGAR AND TURBINADO SUGAR** are made from slightly purified, crystallized evaporated cane juice. They have a trace of the brown molasses coloring and are in a larger crystal form than regular granulated sugar. They have a slightly richer flavor than white granulated sugar. I use the two terms interchangeably throughout the book, however, demerara is known for being slightly darker with a deeper molasses flavor. Either will work for the recipes here. Organic versions and proprietary brands can be found at most larger retailers.

Organic sugars have more color than granulated white cane sugar, but they also bring a bit more flavor to the party.

★ **LIGHT AND DARK BROWN SUGARS** are either unrefined or partially refined sugar crystals with some residual molasses content, or are produced by the addition of molasses to refined white sugar so the ratio of molasses can be carefully controlled. Light brown sugar contains 3.5% molasses; dark brown sugar contains 6.5% molasses. These sugars tend to be softer due to the moisture content of the molasses and have a more robust flavor than granulated white sugar. These are available at most retailers.

★ **STEVIA** is a natural sweetener from the leaves of several species of plants. It has an insignificant effect on blood glucose levels and is therefore useful as a sugar substitute for diabetics and those on carbohydrate-controlled diets. While it was once only available at health food stores, it has become far more readily available in recent years at supermarkets and specialty grocers.

★ **AGAVE NECTAR** is produced from the same plant that tequila is made from. It is sweeter than honey but less viscous. Like stevia, it is a more healthful alternative due to its lesser effect on blood glucose levels. It is often used as a sweetening agent in tequila or mescal-based cocktails because it complements the flavors of the spirit rather than competing with or masking them, while additionally providing some viscosity and "mouth feel" to the drinks. Agave nectar is quite easy to find now as most grocery and health food stores carry at least one brand. Some brands are certified organic, and some brands offer a light, medium, dark, and extra-dark profile, which provide different levels of richness and flavor. Flavored nectars are available and can put a whole new twist on your cocktails.

»» Spices ««

Most of the spices called for in these recipes will be of the whole dried variety, unless otherwise specified. Try to buy organic spices whenever possible, most particularly if they are going to be used in an infusion. Alcohol strips flavors and chemical compounds out of dried spices and fresh herbs. Knowing that the raw materials have never been exposed to pesticides or been irradiated will make you feel more comfortable with the finished product and to feel safe serving it or drinking it.

There are several excellent online sources for organic spices and extracts, many of which are listed in the Resources section on page 151.

»» Market-Fresh Produce: Fruits, Vegetables, and Herbs ««

The easiest way to guarantee that the produce you're purchasing for your creations is the freshest possible is to buy locally and seasonally. Farmers' markets and community-supported agriculture networks are your best resources for produce as well as being an unending source of inspiration. CSA baskets are always filled with surprises, all season long, and there's no better way to arouse creativity than being resourceful.

When buying fresh produce, it is important to know what's in season, and to know what characteristics to look for. Bruising or discoloration, for example, is a sign of poor handling or overripeness. (Although, for some drink recipes, overripe is perfect.)

The texture of the produce should be both appetizing and appropriate for its type. Fruits and vegetables should be intact, without soft spots, browning, or mold. Berries should be firm and not collapsed. Limp carrots or cucumbers, mealy apples or pears, or mushy berries are not at their prime and will not yield the best results.

If you aren't certain what the appropriate texture for ripeness is for what you are purchasing, consult your grocer or produce manager at the supermarket, or the farmer at the farmers' market. They can offer guidance both for purchasing and for storing your purchases appropriately to keep them at their freshest.

Buying fresh herbs is a more delicate proposition. Browned or dried-out leaves should be clipped and discarded before storing. After harvest, tender, fresh herbs can become limp, soggy, and quick to expire in the refrigerator. Here are some tips for keeping your herbs fresh, crisp, and delicious.

★ Rinse fresh herbs well under cool water to remove any dirt or insects. Run through a salad spinner or gently shake off excess water and pat dry *very gently* with paper towels. The essence of the herbs is released by crushing the leaves. If you do it before you're planning to use them, you are wasting valuable aromatics for your recipe.

★ Treat fresh herbs as you would a bouquet of fresh flowers. Cut off the excess stems on an angle and then place them in a glass or vase filled with cool water. Keep the leaves of the herbs above the rim of the container and do not submerge them. Refrigerate (vase and all) and change the water if it becomes cloudy. Clip any leaves that turn yellow or brown.

★ Certain herbs have *trichomes*, appendages or hairs on the leaves that contain the volatile oils that give the herb its flavor. Herbs with a peach-like fuzzy texture such as mint and sage are good examples. These herbs can be stored upside down in ice water, preserving the delicate, volatile oil droplets on the leaf surface. This technique does not keep these herbs fresh indefinitely, but it certainly extends their life.

SEASONAL FIX

You cannot have everything you desire at your disposal in every season. If you have an abundance of something *now*, then take the time to cook it down to preserve it. Many of the recipes in this book freeze well or are shelf-stable either at room temperature or refrigerated. You can preserve your favorite produce while they are at their peak of tastiness so you can indulge out of season. The sweetness of a perfect summer strawberry in the middle of January is awe-inspiring. If you are in tune with the seasons and you preserve your favorite flavors at their peak, you won't ever have a day without a mouth-watering indulgent libation of some sort.

»» Miscellaneous Ingredients ««

There are a few ingredients used in these recipes that might not be available at your regular supermarket.

★ **TARTARIC ACID POWDER** is a food-grade preservative that is available at home-brewing and wine-making shops. You can use it in cooked fruit cordials to give them longer shelf life when refrigerated and also to give the cordial a tart flavor.

★ **CITRIC ACID POWDER** provides acidity in pickling and preserving and has some preservative qualities. It can generally be found at good spice purveyors or some supermarkets listed as "sour salt."

★ **ORANGE FLOWER WATER,** or orange blossom water, is a clear, perfumed distillation of fresh bitter-orange blossoms. It is traditionally used as a flavoring in French and Middle Eastern desserts. Behind the bar, it is used as an ingredient in certain classic cocktails like the Ramos Gin Fizz as well as a flavoring agent in grenadine and cooked fruit cordials.

★ **ROSEWATER** is a byproduct of extracting rose oil from crushed rose petals for perfume. It has a very distinctive flavor and is used as a flavoring agent in many Middle Eastern cuisines as well as in Moroccan couscous and Indian sweets. It is also used as a perfume in Muslim and Zoroastrian religious ceremonies.

★**POMEGRANATE MOLASSES** is a reduced version of pomegranate juice. It is used as a traditional ingredient in Persian cuisine as well as an ingredient in homemade grenadine.

CHAPTER 2 | SYRUPS

Flavored syrups are the easiest way to add new flavors and zip to your cocktails. Most bars that pride themselves on a creative cocktail menu make at least a few different flavored syrups in house that make their cocktails distinctively their own. These are easily made at home. The basis for all flavored syrups is simple syrup, granulated sugar dissolved into water. It is, as the name implies, quite simple to prepare.

Simple syrup is used to counterbalance the acidity in cocktails made with citrus juices and is an essential ingredient in such classic drinks as daiquiris and mojitos as well as an "adjustment" ingredient in most any cocktail that turns out too tart or bitter.

There are plenty of arguments about the best methodology for making simple syrup, as well as the ratios of sugar to water. Some argue that the "cold method" of shaking superfine sugar into water until dissolved is best, while others swear by heating the water/sugar mixture and simmering the syrup. Except when tight for time, I find that the cooked method gives a better end result with a bit more viscosity that I find translates to more texture in the final cocktail.

The one-to-one ratio (by volume, **not** by weight) of sugar to water works best when making simple syrup. It's a known quantity and most cocktail recipes are geared to this metric. While a "rich," simple syrup of two or more parts sugar to one part water might be useful for certain applications, remember that this version of the syrup is sweeter and you'll need less of it in a drink to achieve a balanced end result.

4 cups (1 L) sugar
4 cups (1 L) water
optional: 1 ounce 100 proof vodka for preservation

1. Combine the sugar and water in a saucepan and bring to a simmer. Stir or whisk gently until the sugar dissolves and simmer for one more minute once combined.
2. Remove from the heat and allow it to cool to room temperature.
3. Add optional vodka, if using.
4. Transfer to a clean bottle or container. Simple Syrup keeps refrigerated for up to a month, longer in the colder back area of your fridge.

★ **YIELD: 1 QUART (1 L)** ★

{ Add some refrigerated shelf stability and longevity to your syrups by adding a small amount of vodka to them. A 100-proof vodka is particularly useful. It won't change the flavor and will retard bacterial growth or fermentation. I recommend a ratio of approximately one half tablespoon per cup (7 ml per 235 ml), so one ounce per quart (28 ml per litter) of finished syrup. If you plan on using your syrup up immediately, you can feel free to skip this step. }

DEMERARA SIMPLE SYRUP

Demerara Simple Syrup is made by simply replacing the white granulated sugar in the Simple Syrup recipe (above) with demerara sugar. Demerara sugar is similar to turbinado sugar in that it is less refined, has larger, irregularly-shaped crystals, and still has some color to it. It retains a more robust molasses-like flavor and tastes a bit richer than the one-dimensional "sweetness" of regular white, refined sugar. A spoonful of plain simple syrup would merely be sweet, whereas demerara or turbinado simple syrup has sweetness and a distinctive flavor to it. I tend to use the terms demerara and turbinado almost interchangeably, although there are slight differences in taste (demerara has notes of molasses, while turbinado is said to contain hints of honey) and texture (demerara crystals are slightly larger). Both are less refined, more natural sugars than the usual supermarket stuff and make for a more complex and richer tasting simple syrup that I recommend for some of the recipes in this book.

STORING SIMPLE SYRUPS

Most syrups freeze well. They can be poured into large, airtight plastic containers (such as the ones used for takeout soups), labeled, and dated. Like any other food item you would freeze, however, using your syrup sooner rather than later is best.

The more delicate herbal and floral flavors might suffer most from being frozen and defrosted; there will be less natural degradation of flavor the sooner you freeze the syrup after making it. Don't let that lovely syrup sit in the refrigerator for two weeks until you realize you need that shelf space back and its flavor is fading. Freeze any excess immediately or as soon as you realize you won't be using it quickly.

{ A neat trick is to pour a syrup into ice cube trays, freeze it, and pop the cubes into a big zip-top freezer bag. Label and date the bag and defrost the cubes on an as-needed basis. This works very well if you're one of those lucky folks with a DBR—or Dedicated Beverage Refrigerator—in your basement or garage where you keep beer, sodas, and wine for entertaining. }

SWEET SUBSTITUTIONS

{ It's also easy to vary the flavoring effect syrups will have on a cocktail by changing the sweetening agent used to make it. Substituting turbinado sugar for refined white sugar will give a richer and more molasses-flavored end result. Substituting honey or agave nectar for sugar will give a different flavor. Use a lighter hand with these, as they tend to be sweeter and far more viscous than regular sugar. If, like many of us, you're concerned about calories and carbohydrates, stevia might be a good alternative for "skinny" cocktail syrups. Be very careful with this, as stevia is exponentially sweeter than regular granulated sugar. Replacing up to half of the sugar with stevia is far more successful than trying to use stevia exclusively. Stevia brands vary in the volume necessary to equal a set volume of sugar, so read labels carefully. }

HERBAL, SPICED, AND FRUIT SYRUPS

Simple syrup becomes way more interesting and more than just a sweetening agent when you add herbs, spices, or fruits to the mix. Here's where the creativity begins. Virtually any fresh herb, dried spice, or fresh or dried fruits can be made into simple syrup to enhance your cocktails or nonalcoholic beverages. It's no more complicated than steeping a cup of tea.

Gently blanch fresh or dried herbs in simmering simple syrup and then let the power of the blender break up the flavoring agent into small bits while the syrup is still hot, so more surface area is exposed. The syrup then cools as the flavor steeps into the syrup. (It's like making a batch of sticky-sweet tea.) You may think this is being a little rough with the ingredients, but it certainly extracts every last ounce of flavor into the syrup. Unlike over-salting soup, you *can* undo overly strong syrup by diluting it with more plain simple syrup.

{ The flavors of fresh herbs may vary from week to week during the growing seasons, and fresh fruit may be sweeter or tarter in any given season. Rely on your own palate to adjust the strength of flavor in your syrups. }

SAFETY TIP: Always let the syrup cool for a short while before buzzing them through the blender. And remember that the laws of physics will dictate that hot syrup in your blender container will *expand* as you run it. *Always remove the tiny pour-through cap, hold a towel on the lid of the blender container when you start it, and start at the lowest speed first.* I have cleaned sticky dripping syrup raining down off of the ceiling of my kitchen. I'd love to say I only made that mistake once, but after the second time it happened, I most decidedly learned this lesson.

★ HERBAL SYRUPS ★

Herbal syrups are simple to prepare and the only real variation is the amount of herb needed for each recipe. Strongly flavored herbs such as rosemary and lavender require less of the raw materials than more delicately flavored herbs like thyme or mint. As when cooking with herbs, I never recommend allowing syrups to come to a full boil once fresh herbs are added, because the herbs can turn bitter. Other than that, once the technique is mastered, the possibilities are virtually endless.

Thai basil is a deliciously fragrant herb that works well in cocktails as well as Thai cuisine.

THAI BASIL SYRUP

Thai basil combines the pungent and familiar flavor of traditional Italian basil with a minty note that works really well in cocktails. It is both savory and refreshing all at once. This syrup is bright screaming green when it's finished and brings that color to whatever cocktail it is added to.

2 cups (475 ml) Simple Syrup (page 34).
1 cup (80 g) Thai basil leaves, rinsed clean and patted dry (a)

1. Bring Simple Syrup to a boil in a medium-size pot. Blanch basil leaves in syrup for 1 to 2 minutes. Turn off the heat and let it cool slightly (b, c).
2. Pour mixture into the blender (d).
3. Pulse the syrup in the blender in small batches to expose maximum surface area (e, f, g). REMEMBER: Hot liquids expand. *Always* hold a towel over the blender when blending.
4. Cool the syrup to room temperature and transfer to a smaller food-safe container. Refrigerate overnight.
5. Strain the syrup carefully the next day to remove leafy particles (h). Transfer to a food-safe container or a sterile glass bottle and keep refrigerated. Keeps for up to 1 month refrigerated or can be frozen for up to 6 months.

★ YIELD: 2 CUPS (475 ML) ★

Front Stoop Lemonade

The name of the cocktail stems from the architectural reality of Philadelphia where people have neither front nor back porches, but only front stoops, where folks will often sit on a hot summer night and have a drink with their friends and neighbors.

1 ounce (30 ml) Thai Basil Syrup (opposite)
2 ounces (60 ml) gin (I use Bluecoat*)
1 ounce (30 ml) Lemon Cordial (see Chapter 3, page 103)
Splash fresh lemon juice
Club soda

Build over ice in a collins glass.
1. First add bright green Thai Basil Syrup and gin to your glass to form the foundation of the Front Stoop Lemonade (a).
2. Add fresh Lemon Cordial to create the base lemonade flavoring to the drink (b).
3. Add the freshly squeezed lemon juice for acidity and to add brightness to the cocktail (c). Toss (pour back and forth between two glasses) to mix, fill with soda, and stir.
4. Top the mixture with soda to lighten and slightly carbonate your cocktail (d). Stir to combine.
5. Garnish with a lemon wheel and a Thai basil leaf.

*Bluecoat Gin is produced by Philadelphia Distilling Company, and has a more citrus-forward flavor that is particularly well-suited to this cocktail. You can experiment with your favorites for personal variations.

★ **YIELD: ONE DRINK** ★

a   b   c   d

MINT SYRUP

One problem with drinks that contain muddled herbs is that often the herbs are overmuddled, which releases chlorophyll and bitter flavors, rather than just the volatile oils on the surface of the leaves. To prove this theory, gently rub a mint leaf between two fingers and sniff the results. Now rub a leaf until it's destroyed and smell the result. Preparing mint syrup instead of muddling herbs solves this problem and makes the drinks more consistent as well.

1 cup (80 g) loosely packed mint leaves, removed from stems
2 cups (475 ml) simmering Simple Syrup

1. Rinse mint leaves in cool running water. Shake off excess water and add to Simple Syrup.
2. Blanch leaves in syrup for a minute or two and then turn off the heat and cool slightly.
3. Puree syrup and leaves through the blender and allow to cool overnight in the fridge.
4. Strain carefully through a fine-mesh strainer the next day, stirring and pressing down on the solids with a spoon to get all the syrup strained away from the leaf puree.

Mint syrup keeps refrigerated for about 1 week.

★ **YIELD: APPROXIMATELY 2 CUPS (475 ML)** ★

Fresh mint always adds a fresh
and lively note to cocktails.

Mojito

Ernest Hemingway certainly knew how to drink well, and he was a big fan of the Mojito. The mojito is one of the most well-known rum highball drinks, and we have Cuba to thank for this refreshing and delicious beverage. While the exact history of the cocktail is a bit *muddled*, it is fairly certain that the mint, lime, and sugar were meant to both complement the flavor of the rum as well as smooth out any harsh edges in the potent spirit.

In Cuba, *guarapo* or sugar cane juice is used rather than sugar, and a particular type of mint called *yerba buena* is preferred. Using your own mint syrup makes the drink consistent both in the level of mint flavor as well as the level of sweetness. You can make easy variations of mojitos by trying different flavored rums in the drink.

Mojitos are one of the most popular rum cocktails in the world.

One quarter of a lime, cut into wedges
½ teaspoon turbinado sugar
¾ ounce (22 ml) Mint Syrup (opposite)
½ ounce (15 ml) fresh lime juice
2 ounces (60 ml) white rum
Club soda or lime-flavored seltzer

1. Muddle lime wedges with turbinado sugar, using the gritty sugar as an abrasive to get some of the oils out of the lime peels.
2. Add mint syrup, fresh lime juice, and rum over the muddled lime wedges and sugar. Top with ice and shake vigorously. Pour contents into a highball or collins glass.
3. Top with more ice to fill and a splash of club soda or seltzer.
4. Stir and garnish with a mint sprig you have "spanked" or clapped between your palms to release the oils so you can smell the mint as you bring the glass to your lips.

★ YIELD: ONE DRINK ★

Smoked Peach Bourbon Smash

The standard, old-school definition of a "smash" cocktail is essentially a julep with some fruit added to it. This variation adds a smoky flavor dimension and plays up the natural affinity of peaches and bourbon.

Half of a smoked peach* (and a bit of the juice from the smoker container)
1 ounce (30 ml) Mint Syrup (page 40)
2 ounces (60 ml) bourbon
¾ ounce (22 ml) fresh lemon juice
Dash peach or orange bitters

1. Muddle the peach half in the Mint syrup in bottom of shaker until well destroyed.
2. Add bourbon, lemon juice, bitters, and ice and shake vigorously.
3. Double-strain into a rocks glass over fresh ice.
4. Garnish with a lemon wheel or peach wedge.

* Peaches are smoked for 20 minutes according to manufacturer's instructions on stove or grill top with wood chips of your choice. It is best to do these a day ahead and allow them to sit overnight in the refrigerator so they can rest and give up some of their juices.

★ **YIELD: ONE DRINK** ★

Peaches are at their height of sweetness in the summer months, and have a natural affinity for bourbon. Try them with mint for a divine pairing.

Mint Julep

Mint Juleps are a refreshing classic that are delicious all year.

The classic Mint Julep is as refreshing as can be on a hot summer day. It's like a grown-up snow cone of bourbon and minty goodness. Try drizzling peach syrup on top as well (see page 80).

1 ounce (30 ml) Mint Syrup (page 40)
2 ½ ounces (75 ml) bourbon
Crushed ice
Garnish: Mint sprig
Optional: Drizzle of Peach Syrup (page 80)

1. Stir Mint Syrup and bourbon together in shaker.
2. Pack crushed ice in a silver julep cup or rocks glass until mounded slightly over the top.
3. Pour mint and bourbon mixture over the crushed ice.
4. Drizzle peach syrup over top of ice if desired.
5. Garnish with a large sprig of mint that has "spanked" or clapped between your palms to release the fragrant oils.

★ **YIELD: ONE DRINK** ★

ROSEMARY SYRUP

Rosemary is stronger than most other herbs, so pulsing it through the blender is not necessary or recommended for some palates. If you do blend it, remove the leaves from the woody stems first, and use fewer leaves, approximately one-quarter cup (60 ml) per two cups (475 ml) of Simple Syrup. I prefer to bruise the sprigs instead, simmer them gently, and then allow them to steep and cool before straining.

2 cups (475 ml) simmering Simple Syrup (page 34)
8 sprigs of rosemary, bruised with a rolling pin or roughly chopped with a chef's knife

1. Add rosemary sprigs to simmering syrup. Simmer for 10 minutes.
2. Allow to cool and steep overnight in the fridge.
3. Strain and funnel into a clean, sterilized bottle for storage.

Keeps for approximately 1 month refrigerated.

★ **YIELD: APPROXIMATELY 2 CUPS (475 ML)** ★

Fresh rosemary is easy to grow and works well in cocktails as well as cuisine.

Rosemary Lemonade (courtesy of Andrea Fleegle)

This nonalcoholic drink is super refreshing and savory at the same time. If you wish to make an alcoholic cocktail version, adding a couple of ounces of citrus vodka or gin to the mix works very well.

4 ounces (120 ml) Rosemary Syrup (above)
4 ounces (120 ml) Simple Syrup (page 34)
8 ounces (240 ml) fresh lemon juice
Water or club soda
Garnish: Lemon wheel

1. Combine the syrups and lemon juice to create a concentrate.
2. Mix 3–4 ounces (90 to 120 ml) concentrate with an equal volume of water or club soda and stir to mix for plain or sparkling lemonade. Add spirits if desired.
3. Add lemon wheel for garnish.

★ **YIELD: 1 QUART (1 L)** ★

Rosemary Paloma (courtesy of Jamie Boudreau)

The paloma is one of the better known non-margarita tequila cocktail variations. It's very popular in Mexico, where it is usually made with a grapefruit-flavored soda rather than fresh grapefruit juice and club soda. This version, from Seattle-based bartender and host of Small Screen Network's *Raising the Bar* Jamie Boudreau, adds the herbaceous rosemary flavor to its already refreshing mix. A pinch of salt is sometimes added to the paloma, whose name means "dove" in Spanish. You could also half rim the glass with salt like a Margarita, so you can alternately take sips with and without salt, if desired.

3 ounces (90 ml) blanco tequila
2 ounces (60 ml) fresh grapefruit juice
½ ounce (15 ml) fresh lime juice
½ ounce (15 ml) Rosemary Syrup
1 ounce (30 ml) chilled club soda
Garnish: Grapefruit wheel and sprig of rosemary (a)

1. Fill a cocktail shaker with ice. Add the tequila, grapefruit juice, lime juice, and Rosemary Syrup and shake well.
2. Strain into an ice-filled highball glass and stir in the club soda (b).
3. Garnish with a grapefruit wheel and sprig of rosemary.

★ **YIELD: ONE DRINK** ★

Rosemary, grapefruit, and lime are the savory building blocks for the Rosemary Paloma.

a

b

THYME SYRUP

Thyme is a fairly subtle herb, and the leaves are maddeningly tiny. You can strip the leaves off the stems by gently running them against the grain between two fingers. Or you can just cut the bottom thicker parts of the stems and not worry about it!

2 cups (475 ml) simmering Simple Syrup (page 34)
¾ cup (60 g) thyme sprigs, packed down, bottoms of stems removed

1. Rinse the thyme sprigs and shake dry. Add to syrup and allow to simmer for 5 minutes.
2. Remove from heat and cool slightly.
3. Puree syrup and leaves through the blender and allow to cool overnight in the fridge.
4. Strain carefully through a fine-mesh strainer the next day, gently stirring and pressing down on the solids with a spoon to get all the syrup strained away from the leaf puree.

Keep refrigerated for up to 1 month.

★ **YIELD: APPROXIMATELY 2 CUPS (475 ML)** ★

Parisian Martini

Lillet is an aromatized wine from France that is served as an aperitif. It is used as a cocktail ingredient similar to the way vermouth is used.

2½ ounces (75 ml) gin (I prefer Hendrick's or Bluecoat,
   something with a less juniper-flavor profile)
1 ounce (30 ml) Lillet Blanc
½ ounce (15 ml) fresh lemon juice
½ ounce (15 ml) Thyme Syrup (above)
2 dashes Fee Brothers lemon bitters
Garnish: Orange twist

1. Shake all ingredients together and strain into a chilled cocktail glass.
2. Garnish with a fat orange twist that has had the oils expressed over the cocktail.

★ **YIELD: ONE DRINK** ★

LAVENDER SYRUP

Lavender is a truly unique and delicious flavor, but *only in moderation*. There's a very fine line with lavender where the right amount is lovely, and just a bit too much is like eating the guest soaps. Your tolerance may vary and you might wish to adjust proportions to your own taste. When purchasing lavender for use in cocktails, make certain that it is culinary grade lavender, to be certain it hasn't been treated with anything that might render it inedible.

2 cups (475 ml) simmering Simple Syrup (page 34)
½ cup (40 g) dried lavender

1. Bruise the lavender in a plastic bag with a rolling pin.
2. Add bruised lavender leaves to the syrup and simmer for 10 minutes.
3. Cool overnight and strain.

★ **YIELD: 2 CUPS (475 ML)** ★

Lavender Lemonade

For this recipe, as in the Rosemary Lemonade, the basic proportions of one part flavored syrup, one part plain syrup, and two parts fresh lemon (or lime) juice diluted with an equal proportion of water or soda, remain the same.

This basic recipe works for an almost endless variety of flavored syrups and fruit juices. Pineapple-sage-ade is delicious, as is basil-watermelon-ade. You're only limited by your own imagination.

Using the listed proportions, the end result might be closer to a Mexican *agua fresca* than a more strongly flavored "ade" drink, but you can adjust appropriately. For juices that aren't as tart or strong as lemon or lime, adjust the proportions for less syrup and less dilution and/or add some lemon or lime juice to dial back sweetness according to your own tastes.

4 ounces (120 ml) Lavender Syrup (above)
4 ounces (120 ml) plain Simple Syrup (page 34)
8 ounces (240 ml) fresh lemon juice
Water or club soda
Garnish: Lemon wheel

1. Combine the syrups and lemon juice to create a concentrate.
2. Mix 3–4 ounces (90 to 120 ml) concentrate with an equal volume of water or club soda and stir to mix for plain or sparkling lemonade.

★ **YIELD: 4 OR 5 SERVINGS, DEPENDING ON HOW STRONG IT IS** ★

Provençal Martini

Lavender and gin go together like bread and butter. This is a variation of the Parisian Martini made with Thyme Syrup.

2½ ounces (75 ml) gin
1 ounce (30 ml) Lillet Blanc
½ ounce (15 ml) fresh lemon juice
½ ounce (15 ml) Lavender Syrup (page 47)
2 dashes Fee Brothers lemon bitters
Garnish: Lemon twist

1. Shake and strain ingredients into a chilled cocktail glass.
2. Garnish with a fat lemon twist that has had the oils expressed over the cocktail.

★ **YIELD: ONE DRINK** ★

The Provençal Martini is a modern take on a classic French martini that combines gin, lavender, and lemon to an elegant effect.

HONEYSUCKLE SYRUP (courtesy of Barbie Marshall)

2 cups (475 ml) water
1 cup (235 g) granulated sugar
2 ounces (20 g) honeysuckle flowers (a large handful)
One lemon wedge (⅛ of a lemon), squeezed
Pinch of cinnamon

1. Bring the water and sugar to a boil. Allow to cool slightly.
2. Add remaining ingredients and steep until cooled to room temperature.
3. Pour into a clean storage bottle and refrigerate.

This syrup, when refrigerated, keeps for approximately 3 months.

NOTE: The squeeze of lemon is to prevent the crystallization of the sugar and the pinch of cinnamon enhances the honeysuckle flavor. In both cases, just the slightest amount will do.

★ YIELD: APPROXIMATELY 2 CUPS (475 ML) SYRUP ★

Fragrant honeysuckle blossoms bloom in the late spring and occasionally a second time in autumn. The beautiful bell-shaped flowers contain a sweet nectar that can be infused into a delicately flavored syrup for cocktails.

Honeysuckle Syrup not only tastes delicious, but looks beautiful when it's finished.

The GMF (courtesy of Barbie Marshall and Ian Brendle, Green Meadow Farm, Gap, Pennsylvania)

Green Meadow Farm provides fresh seasonal specialty produce and herbs to many of Philadelphia and Lancaster's finest restaurants. Barbie, who is a trained chef, and Ian, who runs the farm with his father, Glenn, created this cocktail to showcase the flavors of the delicious late summer melons and the fragrant honeysuckle syrup. The intermingling of the sweet flavors with the botanicals in the gin are delightfully intoxicating.

1 ounce (30 ml) canary, honeydew, or cantaloupe melon puree
½ ounce (15 ml) Honeysuckle Syrup (page 49)
1 ounce (30 ml) gin
1–2 ounces (30 ml to 60 ml) club soda, to taste
Garnish: Lemon wheel or wedge, or a fresh, rinsed honeysuckle blossom if available

1. Pour the melon puree, Honeysuckle Syrup, and gin over ice in a cocktail shaker.
2. Shake vigorously until well chilled, and pour over fresh ice in a rocks glass.
3. Top with club soda to taste, stir, and garnish as desired.

NOTE: Like the watermelon puree, this melon puree should be made as close to serving time as possible. Barbie suggests when pureeing the peeled, seeded, and diced melon flesh in the blender, adding a small pinch of salt to bring out the flavor.

★ **YIELD: ONE DRINK** ★

Canción de Flores

This cocktail is a bit of a cross between a margarita and a mimosa, marrying flavor elements from both. The tequila is well accentuated by the flavor of the fragrant honeysuckle syrup, and the citrus juices add enough acidity to keep the drink from becoming cloying.

1 ounce (30 ml) reposado tequila
¾ ounce (22 ml) Honeysuckle Syrup (page 49)
½ ounce (15 ml) fresh lime juice
½ ounce (15 ml) fresh orange juice
Chilled champagne or sparkling wine
Garnish: Orange wedge or curl or zest

Canción de Flores is a delicious alternative cocktail to serve for brunch when you've grown tired of the usual Bloody Marys and mimosas.

1. Pour the tequila, Honeysuckle Syrup, lime and orange juices over ice in a cocktail shaker.
2. Shake until well chilled and strain into a champagne flute.
3. Top with champagne and garnish with an orange wedge or a long curled orange zest.

★ **YIELD: ONE DRINK** ★

HIBISCUS SYRUP

Hibiscus has a lovely sweet-tart flavor and a gorgeous color. Hibiscus is used as the basis for beverages and as a vegetable dye in many cultures. Hibiscus teas, both hot and cold, are popular in Mexico, where it is known as *Jamaica* (ha-MAI-ca), and in the Caribbean where it's known as sorrel. It's simple to make and works in many different applications, both alcoholic and nonalcoholic.

6 cups (1.4 L) water
3 cups (240 g) loosely packed, dried hibiscus flowers
5 cups (1.2 L) sugar
1 tablespoon (15 ml) pure vanilla extract (optional)
1 teaspoon pumpkin pie spice (also optional, but works well in several of the cocktail recipes)

1. Bring water to boiling in a large pot and remove from heat.
2. Stir dried hibiscus flowers into the water gently, cover, and allow to cool for several hours or overnight.
3. Strain out the now rehydrated hibiscus flowers.
4. Bring hibiscus water back to a simmer and add sugar, whisking until dissolved, and remove from heat.
5. Add vanilla extract and spice if desired, stirring to be certain all ingredients are fully incorporated.

Store in refrigerator for up to 1 month, or freeze up to 6 months.

{ You can save the whole rehydrated hibiscus flowers in Hibiscus Syrup to cover for the following cocktail, as a drink garnish, or just to enjoy their tart raspberry-like flavor. They are completely edible and quite delicious. }

★ YIELD: APPROXIMATELY 2 QUARTS (2 L) ★

Love in Bloom

A small amount of Hibiscus Syrup topped with champagne and a flower in the glass and you have a beautiful looking and tasting romantic cocktail. It's important to use a very dry sparkling wine so the acidity and dryness of the sparkling wine balances the sweet syrup and the end result cocktail isn't too sweet and cloying.

1 rehydrated hibiscus flower
½–¾ ounce (15 ml to 22 ml) Hibiscus Syrup to taste (page 51)
4 ounces (120 ml) Brut champagne or dry sparkling wine of your choice

1. Place hibiscus flower at the bottom of a champagne flute.
2. Top with Hibiscus Syrup.
3. Gently pour sparkling wine down the side of the flute until almost filled. The bubbles in the wine should help the flower "bloom" at the bottom of the flute, and the wine should have turned a lovely shade of pink in the glass.

★ **YIELD: ONE DRINK** ★

Love in Bloom is both pretty and delicious and a romantic cocktail for a special occasion.

Man-Full-O'-Trouble Punch

This drink is named after an historical colonial tavern in Philadelphia. I'd like to think the structure and many of the ingredients in the recipe are close enough to a true colonial-style punch that it might have been served proudly to the patrons there many years ago.

2 quarts (2 L) cranberry-pomegranate tea (I use Stash brand), brewed and cooled
1 bottle (1¾ L) cognac
1 cup (235 ml) Grand Marnier liqueur
½ cup (120 ml) apple brandy (I use Laird's Bonded)
½ cup (120 ml) cranberry or pomegranate juice
½ cup (120 ml) sweet vermouth (Carpano Antica or sweet vermouth of choice)
2 cups (475 ml) Hibiscus Syrup (page 51)
½ cups (120 ml) sugar, dissolved into lemon juice
2½ cups (590 ml) fresh lemon juice
48 ounces (1½ L) ginger ale

1. Mix together all ingredients except for ginger ale in a large container.
2. Divide into 3 approximately half-gallon (2 L) batches.
3. Place each batch into a punch bowl and add 16 ounces (475 ml) ginger ale just before serving, so the punch doesn't go flat.
4. To serve, ladle 5 ounces (150 ml) punch over ice in a wine glass or punch cup. Garnish with a lemon slice or a hibiscus flower on a skewer/pick.

This punch works really well with a very large block of ice so it doesn't get too diluted, but stays cold.

★ YIELD: 1½ GALLONS (5.7 L), ENOUGH FOR APPROXIMATELY 48 FIVE-OUNCE (150 ML) SERVINGS ★

{ An easy way to make block ice is to use a rinsed out half gallon milk carton with the top cut off. You can even freeze it in stages with lemon slices tucked down the sides so it looks really pretty when unmolded with a hot towel and dropped into your punch bowl. If you're feeling less like a perfectionist about it, plastic quart containers make for nice large blocks of ice for punch, too. }

MIXED HERB SYRUP

This delicious syrup goes well with so very many things I'm hard pressed to think of an application in which it hasn't worked. For nonalcoholic beverages it's delicious for sweetening iced tea or lemonade, and for cocktails it's delicious in a highball with almost any spirit, a splash of lemon or lime, and the clear carbonated mixer of your choice. It's tasty with club soda, ginger ale, tonic water, bitter lemon, and grapefruit sodas, depending on how sweet or dry you want your end cocktail to be. This can be handy for a party if you want to have a variety of drinks available with the least amount of active bar maintenance. Keep the syrup in a squeeze bottle on ice or refrigerated in a small pitcher, provide a stocked bar and a variety of carbonated mixers, and you've got a party.

3 cups (710 ml) simmering Simple Syrup (page 34)
½ cup (40 g) packed mint leaves
¼ cup (20 g) packed basil leaves
¼ cup (20 g) packed cilantro leaves

1. Rinse the herbs and pat dry gently.
2. Add to syrup and allow to simmer for 5 minutes.
3. Remove from heat and cool slightly. Puree syrup and leaves through the blender and allow to cool overnight in the fridge.
4. Strain carefully through a fine-mesh strainer the next day, gently stirring and pressing down on the solids with a spoon to get all the syrup strained away from the leaf puree.

Keep refrigerated.

★ **YIELD: APPROXIMATELY 3 CUPS (710 ML)** ★

Basic Herbal Cooler

The Basic Herbal Cooler is an incredibly versatile recipe. Variations are only limited by what you want to stock your bar with that day. Flavor combinations can be adapted to suit almost every taste. For a sweeter drink use a sweeter mixer such as lemon-lime or grapefruit soda. If you prefer a drier drink mix, with ginger ale or club soda. If you like things with a bitter edge, use bitter lemon or tonic as the mixer. You can adjust the balance of syrup to citrus to your own preferences, but it's best to begin with even proportions.

2 ounces (60 ml) spirit of choice
¾ ounce (22 ml) Mixed Herb Syrup (opposite)
¾ ounce (22 ml) lemon or lime juice
3–4 ounces (90 ml to 120 ml) chilled mixer

1. Pour your chosen spirit, herb syrup, and citrus juice over ice in a collins or highball glass.
2. Top with mixer of your choosing and stir to make certain all the ingredients are well incorporated.

★ **YIELD: ONE DRINK** ★

Basic Herbal Cooler + Spirit + Citrus + Mixer variations:

★ **Rum-Lime-Ginger ale**   ★**Vodka-Lemon-Club soda**
★ **Gin-Lime-Tonic**   ★ **Bourbon-Lemon-Bitter lemon**
★ **Tequila-Lime-Fresca (grapefruit)**

Spice syrups require a different treatment than herbal syrups. You're generally using dried seeds, bark, fruit, or roots rather than fresh leafy substances. Spices are often much stronger in flavor than fresh herbs and smaller quantities will flavor the same volume of syrup. Rather than pureeing the flavoring agent into the syrup, you will generally just simmer the ingredients in to the syrup to flavor it.

DESSERT SPICED SYRUP

This basic formula for a "spiced" syrup contains most of the spices our palates associate with dessert—cinnamon, cloves, allspice, anise, and also just a hint of heat from black pepper and chili flakes. It works in many drinks (it is especially delicious in sangria) and brings a warm and savory character to whatever it touches.

3 cups (710 ml) water
6 cinnamon sticks, broken up
18 whole cloves
4 star anise
12 allspice berries
12 black peppercorns
¼ teaspoon red chile flakes
3 cups (710 ml) sugar

1. Bring the water to a boil in a small saucepan and add the spices. Allow to boil for 3 minutes.
2. Add the sugar and stir to dissolve. Lower heat and allow the syrup to simmer for 10 minutes, stirring occasionally.
3. Turn off the heat and allow it to cool to room temperature. Strain out spices before using and funnel into clean glass bottles for storage. Refrigerate for up to 1 month.

★ YIELD: APPROXIMATELY 3 CUPS (710 ML) SYRUP ★

The Mumbai Mule is a twist on the classic Moscow Mule featuring pomegranate and ginger.

Mumbai Mule

I created this cocktail after enjoying a pitcher of a nonalcoholic pomegranate-ginger-lime "mixer" that was provided by a local Indian-influenced restaurant. It tasted so good and was so refreshing I had to find a way to create a cocktail that mimicked those flavors. This is a variation of the classic Moscow Mule—vodka, ginger beer, and lime.

1½ ounces (45 ml) pomegranate-flavored vodka
1 ounce (30 ml) pomegranate juice
1 ounce (30 ml) Homemade Ginger Beer Concentrate (page 109)
½ ounce (15 ml) fresh lime juice
¾ ounce (22 ml) Dessert Spiced Syrup (page 57)
Club soda
Ginger ale
Garnish: Lime wedge

1. Add vodka, pomegranate juice, ginger beer concentrate, lime juice, and Spiced Simple Syrup to an ice-filled shaker.
2. Shake until well chilled and pour over fresh ice in a highball or collins glass.
3. Add a splash each of club soda and ginger ale. Stir and garnish with a lime wedge.

★ YIELD: ONE DRINK ★

Naughty Pilgrim

Since the traditional Pilgrims (at least the ones who settled the American colonies) were known for their strict religious habits, I figured a cocktail with any sort of alcohol in it would be naughty enough to earn them a trip to the stocks. This cocktail works either with sugar-cane-juice-based rum or with applejack, which makes it taste a little stronger both alcohol-wise and in apple flavor.

2 ounces (60 ml) rhum agricole or applejack
1 ounce (30 ml) fresh apple cider
¾ ounce (22 ml) fresh lemon juice
½ ounce (30 ml) pear brandy or liqueur
½ ounce (15 ml) Dessert Spiced Syrup (page 57)
1 dash Angostura or classic bitters
Garnish: Lemon peel

1. Shake all ingredients, pour over ice, and strain into a chilled cocktail glass.
2. Garnish with a lemon peel that has had the oils expressed over the top of the drink.

★ YIELD: ONE DRINK ★

Basic Hot Toddy

The spices in the Dessert Spiced Syrup just cry out for a hot beverage in front of a roaring fire. This basic hot toddy recipe will work with different base spirits depending on your preference. This is also the perfect cure for all that ails you when you have a bad cold. It warms you up from the inside out.

1 tea bag or 1 teaspoon of loose tea in a tea ball, your choice
    (I happen to enjoy herbal teas for this application)
2 strips each of orange and lemon rind, studded with a few cloves
6 ounces (180 ml) boiling water
1 ounce (30 ml) Dessert Spiced Syrup (page 56)
1½ ounce (45 ml) rum, brandy or whiskeys of your choice

1. Place tea bag or tea ball into a large mug.
2. Add orange and lemon rinds. Cover with boiling water and steep for 3–5 minutes.
3. Remove tea bag/ball, add spiced syrup and spirit of your choice, and stir to combine.

★ **YIELD: ONE DRINK** ★

CINNAMON SYRUP

Cinnamon syrup is a simpler one-note version of the Dessert Spiced Syrup. It's perfect for creating that sharp heat that only cinnamon has for making drinks taste like dessert.

2 cups (475 ml) water
2 cups (475 ml) sugar
10 cinnamon sticks, broken into pieces

1. Mix water, sugar, and cinnamon sticks in a small saucepan and heat on high until sugar dissolves, then lower heat and simmer for 10 minutes.
2. Allow to cool for at least four hours. Discard cinnamon sticks.
3. Funnel into a clean glass bottle for storage. Refrigerate for up to 1 month.

★ **YIELD: 2 CUPS (475 ML)** ★

Hot Apple Pie

This drink is an easy winter warmer and tastes exactly like a slice of hot apple pie. You could easily leave out the vodka and add a few drops of vanilla extract to make a child friendly/teetotalers version of this if you wished. The bitters add a miniscule amount of alcohol to the drink and could be skipped as well, although the drink is less sweet and better balanced if that is included.

1½ ounces (45 ml) vanilla vodka
¾ ounce (22 ml) Cinnamon Syrup
¼ ounce (7 ml) lemon juice
6 ounces (180 ml) hot apple cider or apple juice
Dash orange bitters
Garnish: Lemon rind studded with cloves, cinnamon stick

1. Add vanilla vodka, cinnamon syrup, lemon juice, and bitters to a heat-proof mug. Pour heated apple cider or juice over to mix.
2. Garnish with clove-studded lemon rind and a cinnamon stick stirrer.

★ **YIELD: ONE DRINK** ★

A Hot Apple Pie is a great way to warm up on a cold night and tastes just like this favorite dessert.

Bark and Blood (courtesy of Maggie Meskey, Salt of the Earth, Pittsburgh, PA)

The unique combination of smoky mescal, vibrant flavor and acidity from the orange juice, aromatic barrel-aged vermouth, sweet port, and savory Cinnamon Syrup make for an unforgettable flavor explosion that is quite unlike any other cocktail. The Bark and Blood cocktail is an elegant and sophisticated drink, reflective of Ms. Meskey's own sophisticated palate and good taste, as well as her formidable skills as a mixologist.

1½ ounces (45 ml) Del Maguey Chichicapa mescal
¾ ounce (22 ml) freshly squeezed orange juice
½ ounce (15 ml) Carpano Antica Formula vermouth
¼ ounce (7 ml) Sandeman's Reserve port
¼ ounce (7 ml) Cinnamon Syrup (page 60)
Garnish: Flamed orange oil

1. Combine all ingredients into a cocktail shaker.
2. Add ice and shake vigorously. Double strain into a cocktail coupe and flame the oil of an orange swath over the drink. (See note.)

★ YIELD: ONE DRINK ★

HOW TO FLAME AN ORANGE PEEL

To flame an orange peel, cut a round piece of zest with pith from the side of an orange. Do not get any orange flesh because it will prevent the zest from squeezing properly. Heat the outside surface gently with the flame of a wooden match (I prefer this to a lighter to avoid the chemicals), bring the flame to the edge of the glass, and squeeze the warmed oils from the zest through the flame from about one inch away. The oils will flame up and caramelize before landing on the surface of the drink.

CARDAMOM-KAFFIR LIME SYRUP

Combining cardamom and kaffir lime was a bit of an experiment. I'd hoped that those flavors would be evocative of Asian or Indian cuisine and happily the flavors all worked together beautifully.

2 cups (475 ml) water
6 cardamom pods
8 kaffir lime leaves, shredded with a chef's knife
2 cups (475 ml) sugar

1. Bring water to boil in a small saucepan on stove top. Add cardamom pods, shredded kaffir lime leaves and sugar.
2. Stir until sugar is dissolved, turn down heat, and simmer for five minutes. Allow to cool for 15 minutes.
3. Pulse in blender two or three times to break open softened cardamom pods and mix the cardamom and leaves throughout the still hot syrup.
4. Allow to cool overnight, then strain carefully through a fine strainer to remove chunks of cardamom and leaf debris.
5. Transfer to clean glass bottles to store. Keeps refrigerated for 2 weeks.

★ **YIELD: APPROXIMATELY 2 CUPS (475 ML)** ★

The Grape Gatsby

The combination of sweet, aromatic, and pungent flavors remind me of Indian cuisine. This cocktail is reminiscent of that and would pair well with an Indian dinner, either as an aperitif or consumed with the meal. Since the measurements are consistently equal or doubled parts, this cocktail is easy to create in large batches ahead for parties, either to be shaken to order or served as a punch.

1½ ounces (45 ml) Bluecoat gin
1½ ounces (45 ml) concord grape juice
¾ ounce (22 ml) fresh lemon juice
¾ ounce (22 ml) Cardamom-Kaffir Lime Syrup (page 63)
Garnish: Lemon wedge or wheel

1. Shake ingredients over ice in a shaker and strain into a rocks glass over fresh ice.
2. Garnish with a small lemon wedge or wheel.

★ **YIELD: ONE DRINK** ★

{ I created the Grape Gatsby for Women Against Abuse, a Philadelphia-based nonprofit agency that provides compassionate, nonjudgmental services ranging from emergency shelter, transitional housing, legal services, advocacy, education, and counseling to women throughout the area. I've supported this worthy cause for the last several years by donating my time and a specialty cocktail to Dish It Up, their annual fundraiser. }

GINGER SYRUP

Ginger is an incredibly familiar, yet still somehow exotic flavor. It evokes thoughts of Asian cuisines, spicy baked goods like gingersnap cookies or gingerbread, and refreshing drinks like ginger ale and ginger beer. It's incredibly popular as a cocktail ingredient because it mixes so well with so many different spirits.

Ginger Syrup introduces that flavor in an instantly mixable and consistent form. As well as being a delicious addition to cocktails, it makes a homemade ginger ale with the addition of club soda or lime seltzer and is great drizzled over fresh berries or mixed into plain or fruit-flavored yogurt.

½ cup (40 g) peeled and thinly sliced ginger
1½ cups (355 ml) sugar
2 cups (475 ml) water

1. Combine the ginger, sugar, and water in a medium saucepan over medium heat. Bring to a simmer, stirring until the sugar dissolves.
2. Lower heat and continue simmering for 20 minutes, then remove from heat and cool completely, allowing the ginger pieces to steep in the syrup.
3. Strain the syrup through a fine strainer. Transfer to a clean glass bottle, and refrigerate.

This syrup keeps refrigerated for 2 weeks, but is best used as quickly as possible, since the flavor begins to lose its sharpness over time.

★ YIELD: APPROXIMATELY 2 CUPS (475 ML) ★

Melon-choly Baby

Ginger often brings to mind thoughts of wintery flavors and warm cookies. I took a 180-degree turn with this cocktail and combined ginger and watermelon for a more summery cocktail combining fragrant gin, the spiciness of ginger, and refreshing sweet watermelon puree. The bitters and lime juice dial back the sweetness of the drink and provide a bit more spice and acidity for depth and balance.

1 ounce (30 ml) gin
1 ounce (30 ml) watermelon puree*
1 ounce (30 ml) Ginger Syrup (opposite)
2 dashes Angostura bitters
½ ounce (15 ml) fresh lime juice
Club soda
Garnish: Watermelon wedge and candied ginger

1. Shake gin, watermelon puree, Ginger Syrup, bitters, and lime juice in an ice-filled shaker and strain into a highball or collins glass over fresh ice.
2. Top with club soda and stir gently to combine.
3. Garnish with a watermelon wedge and candied ginger.

* Watermelon puree should be made as close to serving time as possible, since it separates quickly and does not retain its fresh flavor for very long. Cut seedless watermelon into chunks, puree in the blender, and lightly strain it to remove some of the cellulose fibers.

★ **YIELD: ONE DRINK** ★

Watermelon puree is delicate and doesn't keep as well as some other juices, but can be made right before it's needed and used to delicious effect.

ORANGE-CARDAMOM SYRUP

This Orange-Cardamom Syrup, like the Mixed Herbal Syrup, works in a lot of different applications. The flavor complements both white and brown spirits, and is easy to mix with a base spirit of your choosing and a carbonated mixer to make a variety of highball cocktails.

3 cups (710 ml) water
3 cups (710 ml) sugar
Zest of one orange, removed with a vegetable peeler, orange part only, no white pith
10 cardamom pods

1. Bring water to a boil in a medium saucepan. Add sugar and stir to dissolve.
2. Lower heat and add orange zest and cardamom pods. Simmer for 5 minutes to soften orange rinds and cardamom pods.
3. Cool slightly and add syrup, orange zest, and cardamom to blender. Puree gently and allow to cool to room temperature.
4. Strain carefully to remove orange zest and cardamom pieces. Transfer to a clean glass bottle and refrigerate. This syrup keeps for approximately 1 month.

★ YIELD: APPROXIMATELY 3 CUPS (710 ML) ★

Orange-Cardamom Cooler

Just like the Basic Herbal Cooler earlier in this chapter, the bones of this cocktail are very simple. Use the following formula to spin any number of variations.

Base spirit + Flavored sweetener + Citrus + Mixer

The exotic and savory flavor of the Orange-Cardamom Syrup seems to pair well with many different spirits.

2 ounces (60 ml) spirit of choice
¾ ounce (22 ml) Orange-Cardamom Syrup (above)
¾ ounce (22 ml) lemon or lime juice
3–4 ounces (90 ml to 120 ml) chilled mixer

1. Add ice to a tall collins or highball glass.
2. Add spirit of choice, syrup, and citrus juice.
3. Add mixer and stir thoroughly to combine the flavors.

★ YIELD: ONE DRINK ★

The Orange-Cardamom Cooler has many variations to suit your taste and is a great drink for a party for that reason.

Orange-Cardamom Syrup + Spirit + Citrus + Mixer variations:

★ Vodka-Lemon-Club soda   ★ Gin-Lime-Tonic
★ Bourbon-Lemon-Ginger ale   ★ Tequila-Lime-Sprite
★ Rye whisky-Lemon-Soda

Fruit and vegetable syrups take advantage of whatever is freshest and in season. Consider trying rhubarb and strawberries in spring, blueberries and peaches in summer, and pears in autumn and winter...and so on. These syrups bring a delicious zing of fresh fruity flavors to your creations and allow you to create new original and unique cocktails easily, just by the addition of a new flavor to an old favorite.

RHUBARB SYRUP

4 cups (488 g) diced rhubarb (about 4 large stalks)
2½ cups (595 ml) water
1½ cups (355 ml) sugar
½ tablespoon (4 g) freshly microplaned ginger
⅛ teaspoon (.5 g) Chinese five-spice powder

1. In a medium-size saucepan, cover rhubarb with water and bring to a boil on stovetop.
2. Cover, lower heat, and simmer for approximately 25 minutes, until rhubarb begins to break down. Remove from heat.
3. Stir in remaining ingredients and allow to cool to room temperature.
4. Strain into a bowl through a fine-mesh strainer (or squeeze through cheesecloth) pressing on solids with a spoon to remove as much rhubarb syrup as possible.

★ YIELD: APPROXIMATELY 2½–3 CUPS
(595 TO 710 ML) ★

Rhubarb, lime, and grapefruit are the building blocks for the Rhuby Daiquiri, a twist on the classic Hemingway Daiquiri.

Rhuby Daiquiri

Rhubarb is a much under-appreciated vegetable. I came up with this cocktail after I'd had a slice of rhubarb pie on a trip to Lancaster County, Pennsylvania. It had been some time since I'd tasted rhubarb and I'd forgotten just how much I loved it and wanted to recreate that flavor in a glass. (I can be a bit like a dog with a bone when I get an idea into my head.) It's a rhubarb-flavored twist on a Hemingway Daiquiri, using ruby red grapefruit juice to create a pretty pink drink in the glass.

2 ounces (60 ml) white rum (I prefer rhum agricole from Martinique for this cocktail)
¾ ounce (22 ml) fresh lime juice
¼ ounce (7 ml) Luxardo Maraschino liqueur
¼ ounce (7 ml) Simple Syrup
   (page 34)
¼ ounce (7 ml) Rhubarb Syrup
   (opposite)
1 ounce (30 ml) ruby red grapefruit
   juice (freshly squeezed if pos-
   sible; not from concentrate, if
   store bought)
Dash grapefruit bitters
Garnish: Lime wedge

1. Shake over ice and strain into a cocktail glass.
2. Garnish with a lime wedge.

★ **YIELD: ONE DRINK** ★

Celery Syrup pouring—look closely and you can see the celery seeds.

CELERY SYRUP

Celery has a unique earthy, slightly salty flavor that is naturally refreshing, like cucumber. Celery-flavored soda may sound fairly alien, but it's oddly delicious. This version utilizes both fresh celery puree and celery seeds packs a powerful flavor punch. The small splash of ginger ale dries the soda a bit and adds a touch of spiciness to the end result. The fresh herbal flavor and slight saltiness of the syrup is a natural compliment to gin or tequila as well.

2 cups (488 g) sliced celery (about 4 large ribs)
2½ cups (595 ml) plus 1 tablespoon (15 ml) sugar
½ teaspoon kosher salt
2 cups (475 ml) water, divided
2 tablespoons (10 g) celery seeds, freshly ground or crushed

1. Place celery pieces in the blender with 1 tablespoon of the sugar and the salt, and process until the celery is roughly chopped. Add half the water and puree until liquified. Pour pureed celery into a medium saucepan.
2. Use remaining cup of water to rinse out blender container and then add to saucepan. Add remaining sugar to celery puree and warm the mixture just until the sugar dissolves and it just begins to simmer.
3. Remove from the heat and add the ground/crushed celery seed. Cover and allow to steep until completely cooled.
4. Strain though a cheesecloth-lined fine-mesh strainer into a clean container and place in the refrigerator.

The syrup can be stored for up to 1 month.

To make a nonalcoholic celery soda, add 2 tablespoons (15 ml) of syrup to 1 cup (235 ml) soda water. Add a splash of ginger ale if desired and stir to combine.

★ YIELD: APPROXIMATELY 1 QUART (1 L) ★

Jalisco Cel-Ray

This drink is what I imagine would be served at a delicatessen in Mexico, to accompany your pastrami sandwich.

2 ounces (60 ml) of reposado tequila
1½ ounces (45 ml) Celery Syrup (page 73)
½ ounce (15 ml) fresh lime juice
4 ounces (120 ml) club soda
1 ounce (30 ml) ginger ale
Garnish: Celery leaves or heart, and lime wedge

1. Pour tequila, Celery Syrup, and fresh lime juice over ice in a collins glass.
2. Add club soda and ginger ale and stir until thoroughly mixed.
3. Garnish with celery leaves or a small rib of celery from the heart of the bunch and lime wedge.

You can make a London Cel-Ray by substituting gin and lemon juice into this recipe and garnishing with a lemon wheel with the celery in place of the lime wheel.

★ **YIELD: ONE DRINK** ★

Royster Cup

The original premise of this cocktail was to create one that would pair well with oysters. The Royster is a twist on a traditional Pimm's Cup.

2½ ounces (75 ml) Plymouth gin
1½ ounces (45 ml) Pimm's No. 1 Cup
1 ounce (30 ml) fresh lemon juice
1 ounce (30 ml) egg white
1 ounce (30 ml) Celery Syrup (page 73)
Garnish: Lemon twist and celery heart

1. Shake all ingredients vigorously and strain into two coupe glasses.
2. Garnish with a lemon twist expressed over the surface of the drink and a small rib of celery heart.

★ **YIELD: TWO DRINKS** ★

Jalisco Cel-Ray

PEAR SYRUP

Pears are a favorite fruit of mine. I like them out of hand, with cheese, or just the delicious flavor in a cocktail. While it's easy to purchase pear vodka, making fresh pear syrup makes it easy to create cocktails with different spirit bases.

3 cups (710 ml) water
1½ ounces (45 ml) fresh lemon juice, divided
3 very ripe pears, soft but not mushy
2½ (595 ml) cups sugar
⅛ teaspoon citric acid powder

1. Place the water and 1 ounce (30 ml) lemon juice in a large saucepan on the counter.
2. Core and divide the pears using an apple corer (a).
3. Peel each section carefully (b).
4. Place the pear slices into the acidulated water quickly to prevent them from turning brown (c).
5. Place the saucepan on the stovetop and heat over medium heat until gently simmering. Add sugar and stir until dissolved. Simmer pear slices for 20–25 minutes until very soft (d).
6. Allow the pears and the syrup to cool for 30 minutes.
7. Adds the pears and the syrup to blender (e) and puree thoroughly (f).
8. Allow to cool completely. Strain through a fine-mesh strainer, stirring with a spoon if necessary, or squeeze through a double layer of cheesecloth, to remove all the undesirable fibers. Add fresh lemon juice and citric acid powder and stir well to combine. Transfer to clean glass bottles and refrigerate. Keeps approximately 1 week refrigerated.

★ YIELD: APPROXIMATELY 1 QUART (1 L) ★

Pears go well with everything—cheese, desserts, and especially cocktails!

Pear Blossom

This cocktail is a variation of a plum wine version. The St-Germain liqueur adds a lovely floral note, while the Maraschino liqueur adds a funky bass note, and the cranberry juice adds a hint of tartness and color.

1¾ ounces (52 ml) vodka
¾ ounce (22 ml) Pear Syrup (page 76)
½ ounce (15 ml) fresh lemon juice
¼ ounce (7 ml) pineapple juice
¼ ounce (7 ml) St-Germain liqueur (an elderflower liqueur)
1 bar spoon Luxardo Maraschino liqueur
Splash cranberry juice
Dash Fee Brothers lemon or grapefruit bitters
Garnish: Lemon twist

1. Add vodka, Pear Syrup, lemon juice, pineapple juice, St-Germain, Maraschino liqueur, cranberry juice, and bitters to an ice-filled shaker.
2. Shake vigorously until well chilled, and double strain into a cocktail glass.
3. Garnish by squeezing the lemon twist over the drink to express the oils onto the surface of your cocktail.

★ YIELD: ONE DRINK ★

PEACH SYRUP

Peaches speak to me of summer. There's nothing more delicious than biting into a ripe peach and having the juice run down your arms and your chin. Peach syrup preserves that delicious peak-of-summer flavor and puts it into a form that mixes consistently into a drink and allows you to enjoy that flavor even when peaches aren't in season.

4 large peaches (over-ripe ones are fine), peeled, halved, pitted, and cut into chunks
¾ cup (180 ml) water
1½ cups (355 ml) sugar
¾ ounce (22 ml) fresh lemon juice

1. Bring chopped peaches to a boil with water and sugar in a 3- to 4-quart (3 to 4 L) saucepan over medium heat, covered, stirring occasionally until sugar is dissolved.
2. Reduce heat and simmer, covered, until peaches are very soft and have given off their liquid, about 15 minutes.
3. Remove from heat and cool for 1 hour.
4. Mash peaches lightly with a potato masher. Pour mashed peaches and syrup through a fine sieve into a bowl, pressing on and discarding solids, or strain through cheesecloth, squeezing well to extract all the syrup.
5. Stir in lemon juice and chill, covered, until cold. Transfer to clean glass bottles. This syrup keeps refrigerated for up to 2 weeks.

★ **YIELD: APPROXIMATELY 2 CUPS (475 ML)** ★

Better Bellini

The classic Bellini gets a new flavor twist with a touch of earthy Amaro Averna liqueur, which takes a bit of the cloying sweetness away and adds a new dimension of herbal flavors.

1 ounce (30 ml) Peach Syrup (opposite)
1 teaspoon Amaro Averna liqueur
4 ounces (120 ml) Prosecco or champagne
Garnish: Orange twist

1. Add Peach Syrup and Amaro Averna to the bottom of a champagne flute.
2. Pour Prosecco down the side of the flute until almost filled.
3. Add orange twist for garnish.

★ **YIELD: ONE DRINK** ★

The addition of a small amount of amaro to the classic Bellini makes for a less sweet and more elegant cocktail.

It's important to cut citrus twists right before you need them so the oils remain fresh and you can spray them across the surface of a drink to flavor it

BLUEBERRY SYRUP

Blueberries are loaded with antioxidants, vitamins, minerals, and fiber. That alone is a good enough reason to include them in your diet, but their delicious sweet flavor is the best reason to include them in your beverages, both alcoholic and not.

3 cups (710 ml) water
3 cups (366 g) blueberries, rinsed clean and any visible stems removed
2 cups (400 g) sugar
1 teaspoon grated or microplaned lemon zest

1. Bring water to a boil in a medium saucepan.
2. Add blueberries and lower heat to a simmer. Simmer berries for 10 minutes until they begin to soften.
3. Add sugar and stir until dissolved. Remove from heat and cool slightly.
4. Puree in blender, add lemon zest, and allow to cool to room temperature. Strain into a bowl through a fine-mesh strainer, chinoise, or through a double layer of cheesecloth to remove berry skins, lemon zest, and any stems or leaves.
5. Funnel into clean glass jars and refrigerate. This syrup keeps for up to 3 weeks.

★ **YIELD: APPROXIMATELY 1 QUART (1 L)** ★

Blueberry Lemonade

Berries and lemonade just scream summertime. Blueberry lemonade is refreshing and takes advantage of the bounty of the season. This recipe works brilliantly with raspberry or strawberry syrup, too. You could easily substitute raspberries or strawberries into the Blueberry Syrup recipe in the same proportions and use those syrups for berry lemonade variations.

1½ cups (355 ml) Blueberry Syrup (above)
1½ cups (355 ml) fresh lemon juice
3 cups (710 ml) water
Garnish: Lemon wheel or skewered blueberries

6. Combine Blueberry Syrup, lemon juice, and water in a large pitcher or container. Stir well to combine.
7. Serve over ice and garnish with a lemon wheel or skewered blueberries.
8. If you'd like to make this into Adults Only Lemonade, add a couple of ounces of citrus, raspberry, or vanilla vodka, or a citrus-forward gin like Bluecoat to your glass.

★ **YIELD: 1½ QUARTS (1.4 L)** ★

SMOKED PINEAPPLE SYRUP

Grilling fruit brings out the sweetness in a way that no other method seems to. That was, until I got myself a home smoker. Now I can smoke fruits and vegetables for cocktails and really get that smoky barbequed flavor into a glass. Smoked pineapple was the first experiment, and this is what resulted.

1 large over-ripe pineapple
2 cups (475 ml) water
2 cups (475 ml) sugar

1. Remove leaves from the top of the pineapple. Run a chef's knife carefully down the sides of the pineapple, removing the skin and as little flesh as possible.
2. Set up smoker according to manufacturer's instructions. Slice pineapple into approximately twelve ¾" (2 cm)-thick rings.
3. Place pineapple rings into the smoker set at 200°F (93°C) and smoke for 20 to 25 minutes. The rings should be softened and slightly caramelized at that point.
4. Allow pineapple rings to cool. Bring the water and sugar to a simmer in a medium saucepan until sugar is dissolved. Allow the mixture to cool slightly.
5. Place 6 pineapple rings in a blender container. Add the warm Simple Syrup and carefully puree.
6. Allow to cool completely, then strain into a bowl through a fine-mesh strainer or chinoise to remove pineapple fibers.
7. Funnel into clean bottles or a food-safe container for storage. This syrup keeps refrigerated for about 2 weeks.

★ **YIELD: APPROXIMATELY 2 CUPS (475 ML)** ★

Piña Doble

The name of this cocktail is a play on the word *piña*, which in Spanish refers to both the heart of the agave cactus from which the tequila is distilled, and the pineapple itself, which is also called piña.

2 ounces (60 ml) reposado tequila
¾ ounce (22 ml) Smoked Pineapple Syrup (above)
½ ounce (15 ml) Benedictine
¾ ounce (22 ml) fresh lime juice
Club soda
Garnish: Edge of smoked pineapple or a lime wheel

1. Shake all ingredients except the club soda over ice and strain into a collins or highball glass over fresh ice.
2. Top with club soda and stir to combine.
3. Garnish with a wedge of smoked pineapple or lime wheel.

★ **YIELD: ONE DRINK** ★

PASSION FRUIT SYRUP

Passion Fruit Syrup is used in several classic cocktails, including the original recipe for the Hurricane, before it became that oversweetened, artificially colored version of the French Quarter of New Orleans. It has an intriguing sweet-tart flavor that has no substitute. Look for passion fruit pulp under the Spanish name *maracuya*.

1 cup (235 ml) water
2 cups (475 ml) sugar
1½ cups (183 g) passion fruit pulp (one 14-ounces package frozen pulp), defrosted
½ ounce (15 ml) fresh lemon juice
½ teaspoon (2.5 ml) tartaric acid powder

1. Put water and sugar into a saucepan and boil for 5 minutes, until sugar is well dissolved.
2. Add the passion fruit pulp, lemon juice, and tartaric acid powder. Boil for another 3 minutes then remove from heat. Allow to cool to room temperature.
3. Carefully strain out seeds and pulp, and funnel the mixture into a clean bottle. This syrup keeps refrigerated for up to 1 month.

★ **YIELD: APPROXIMATELY 2 CUPS (475 ML)** ★

Hurricane

The Hurricane was supposedly created by New Orleans tavern owner Pat O'Brien during World War II as a means of getting rid of the abundance of cheap rum he was forced to purchase from his distributors in order to be able to order the quota of whiskey and Scotches he really wanted. The drink caught on, and Pat O'Brien's tavern has been serving it in the French Quarter ever since. Unlike the highly sweetened fruity version seen elsewhere, this version is well balanced by the natural tartness still present in the homemade passion fruit syrup.

1½ ounces (45 ml) light rum
1½ ounces (45 ml) dark rum
1¼ ounces (37 ml) Passion Fruit Syrup (above)
1 ounce (30 ml) fresh orange juice
1 ounce (30 ml) fresh lime juice
¼ ounce (7 ml) Homemade Grenadine (page 94)
Garnish: Cherry and a lime wheel

1. Shake all ingredients in an ice-filled shaker and strain over fresh ice into a tall collins or highball glass.
2. Garnish with a cherry and lime wheel.

★ **YIELD: ONE DRINK** ★

The original version of the Hurricane cocktail features
homemade passion fruit syrup.

The Port Light is a rare whiskey-based tiki drink.

Port Light (courtesy Jeff "Beachbum" Berry's book, *Grog Log*)

This drink is a variation of the traditional whiskey sour, but with a lot more depth of flavor and dimension. It is the 1961 creation of Sandro Conti, then bar manager of the now defunct Kahiki Supper Club of Columbus, Ohio. It's a rare whiskey-based tiki drink, from a place one rarely associates with tiki culture. In its heyday, the Kahiki was a wildly popular Columbus restaurant specializing in Asian and Polynesian cuisine as well as the tiki beverage culture that accompanied it. If you're curious, search online for an image of the Kahiki Supper Club to see this magnificent piece of architecture that is sadly no longer with us.

{ The Kahiki Supper Club may have been the first family friendly "eatertainment" venue to feature interactive entertainment via a simulated rainstorm, complete with claps of thunder, flashes of lightning, and water running down the windows inside the restaurant. }

1 ounce (30 ml) bourbon
1 ounce (30 ml) lemon juice
½ ounce (15 ml) Passion Fruit Syrup (page 86)
½ ounce (15 ml) Homemade Grenadine (page 94)
Garnish: Cherry and lemon wedge

1. Shake ingredients with 1 cup (180 g) crushed ice for 5 seconds and pour into a collins glass.
2. Garnish with a cherry and a lemon wedge.

This drink can also be flash-blended in a blender for a "slushier" texture, if desired.

★ YIELD: ONE DRINK ★

BLACKBERRY SHRUB

Shrubs, or "drinking vinegars," are vinegar-based syrups that are lightly sweetened with sugar or honey. Historically this was a popular method of preserving fruits for the winter, and they were popular in the American colonial era. It can be used as a cocktail ingredient or in a glass of white or sparkling wine for an aperitif. Shrubs can also be used in fruit salsas and in desserts.

6 cups fresh (170 g) or frozen (930 g) blackberries
2 cups (475 ml) white balsamic vinegar
2 ounces (60 ml) balsamic vinegar
2 cups (475 ml) water
2½ cups (595 ml) sugar
Garnish: Sprig of mint

1. Place the berries in a large, wide pot or bowl and mash lightly with a ladle or potato masher. Add vinegars, cover with plastic wrap, and allow to sit at least overnight or up to 3 days, stirring once or twice.
2. Puree berry mixture thoroughly in a blender. Press through a fine-mesh strainer into a large pot, removing seeds and fibrous material. Add water and sugar to the pot and bring mixture to a low simmer. Remove from heat and allow to cool.
3. Funnel cooled shrub into clean, sterilized glass bottles and stopper securely. (Run the glassware through boiling water to sterilize.) Shrub keeps for up to 6 months in the refrigerator (a).

Use as a cocktail ingredient or mix with club soda, flavored seltzer, or ginger ale (one part shrub to six parts water) to taste for a refreshing nonalcoholic beverage (b, c). Garnish with a sprig of mint if desired.

RECIPE NOTES: The basic proportions of three parts fruit to one part vinegar plus one part water plus (approximately) one part sugar works well for most any fruit you'd like to make into a shrub. I like just a little more sugar so I've included that in this basic recipe. Your tastes may vary. The end result should be sweet, but with a decidedly vinegary tang.

Most centuries-old recipes call for apple cider or white vinegar. I like the subtle sweetness of white balsamic, but champagne vinegar or sherry vinegar work wonderfully as well. In addition to all kinds of berries, peaches, apricots, and cherries make wonderful shrubs. Stone fruits just need to be pitted and chopped into small pieces; cherries can be pitted and quartered.

YIELD: APPROXIMATELY 6 CUPS (1.4 L)

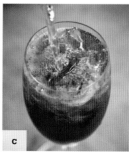

a   b   c

Shrubs are delicious with sparkling water, flavored seltzer,
lemon-lime soda, or ginger ale (one part shrub to six parts
water) for a zingy and refreshing nonalcoholic beverage.

CHAPTER 3

BAR BASICS

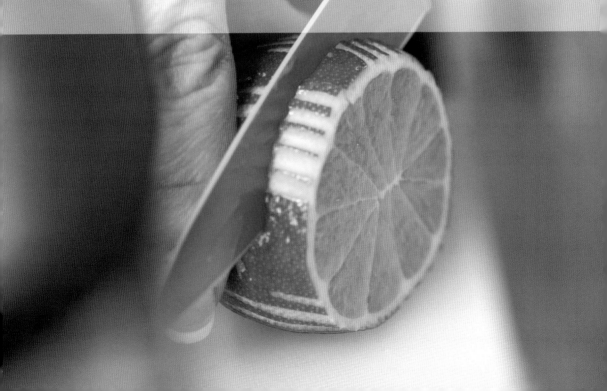

There are several essential ingredients needed to stock your bar for both classic and modern creative cocktails. Rather than relying on store-bought commercial versions of these cocktail mixes that are loaded with artificial colors, flavors, and high-fructose corn syrup, it's easy to make them yourself from fresh ingredients. Like making anything from scratch for yourself or your guests, the end result is one that's far tastier and has origins you know and understand because you controlled it yourself.

★ GRENADINE ★

Grenadine isn't just for "cherry" colas and Shirley Temples. It's a classic cocktail ingredient that is made from pomegranate juice. In fact, the word "grenade" in French means pomegranate, and it's no coincidence that a widely known pomegranate-shaped piece of weaponry goes by the same name. Grenadine is a vibrant red, and is used in cocktails both as a flavoring/ sweetening agent as well as for the color it brings to the drink.

Grenadine at its most basic level is sugar-sweetened pomegranate juice. There are two methods of making it from scratch. "Cold process" involves simply dissolving sugar into pomegranate juice by shaking it hard until all the sugar is incorporated. The "hot process" involves boiling the pomegranate juice until it is concentrated by half and then adding sugar in an equal volume to the original volume of juice. The cold process delivers a "brighter," fresh, and fruity end result. Boiling and reducing the juice concentrates the flavors and creates a richer jam-like syrup as well as a more viscous end result. Since fresh fruitiness and richness are both delicious, I combine both methods to create a best-of-both-worlds final result.

A small amount of pomegranate molasses adds viscosity and acidity, and the orange flower water adds a lovely floral background note. An ounce of overproof vodka makes it shelf stable and helps retard bacterial growth. For this recipe I use pomegranate juice that is not from concentrate, with no sugar added. You may have luck finding this at Eastern European or Middle Eastern markets. Organic unrefined sugar adds some roundness to the finished syrup, but regular white processed sugar will work fine if that is all you have available.

HOMEMADE GRENADINE (COLD PROCESS)

2 cups (475 ml) pomegranate juice
2½ cups (595 ml) organic sugar
2 teaspoons (10 ml) orange flower water (I use Cortas brand)
1 ounce (30 ml) 100 proof vodka
Optional: Scant ⅛ teaspoon (0.5 ml) organic vanilla extract

1. Pour the pomegranate juice into a large container or jar with a tight fitting lid.
2. Gradually add sugar, stirring gently to prevent clumping.
3. Screw on the lid and shake vigorously until all of the sugar has completely dissolved. This requires strong arms and shoulders, but eventually all of the sugar granules will be completely dissolved into the juice.
4. Add the orange flower water and vodka, and the vanilla extract if you're using it, and stir to combine.

HOMEMADE GRENADINE (HOT PROCESS)

2 cups (475 ml) pomegranate juice
2 cups (475 ml) organic sugar
2 ounces (60 ml) pomegranate molasses
Grenadine (from cold process preparation at left)

1. Bring the pomegranate juice to a boil in a medium saucepan over high heat. Turn down the heat to medium and simmer until reduced by half.
2. Slowly add the sugar and whisk until completely dissolved.
3. Add the pomegranate molasses and whisk again to incorporate. Simmer gently for 3 more minutes then remove from heat and allow to cool to room temperature.
4. When the hot syrup has completely cooled, combine it with the cold batch and whisk until the consistency is even.
5. Funnel into clean bottle(s) for storage.

This makes just enough to fill one standard 750 ml wine bottle with perhaps just a bit extra left over. A clean screw-capped wine bottle that has had the label removed and been run through boiling water to sterilize it would be perfect for this purpose.

If you have the extra space, you can keep this refrigerated almost indefinitely. I've kept mine at room temperature on the liquor shelf indefinitely with no ill effect.

★ **YIELD: APPROXIMATELY 25 OUNCES (700 ML) (TOTAL COMBINED)** ★

Jack Rose

The Jack Rose cocktail is a pre-Prohibition classic. It has a notable literary pedigree; it appears in Ernest Hemingway's *The Sun Also Rises*, where the narrator, Jake Barnes, is sipping a Jack Rose in a Paris hotel bar while awaiting the arrival of Lady Brett Ashley. There are many theories on the origin of the name of the drink, from being named after an infamous gambler, an infamous informant in a murder trial, or a hybrid rose. Most likely the name is derived from the plain fact that the drink is made with applejack and is rose colored from the grenadine. It's a simple drink that truly highlights the flavor of homemade grenadine.

Different recipes call for lemon juice or lime juice in this cocktail. That is a matter of preference. I personally prefer lime, but try it both ways to see which you enjoy more.

{ I prefer the Laird's bonded, 100-proof applejack for this drink since it has a stronger apple flavor than the regular blended 80-proof applejack and it can stand up better to the very flavorful homemade grenadine. }

2½ ounce (75 ml) Laird's bonded (100 proof) applejack
¾ ounce (22 ml) fresh lemon or lime juice
½ ounce (15 ml) Homemade Grenadine (page 94)
Garnish: Cocktail cherry (page 124), or lemon or lime twist

1. Shake applejack, citrus juice, and grenadine over ice in a cocktail shaker until well chilled.
2. Strain into a chilled cocktail or coupe glass.
3. Garnish with your choice of garnish.

★ YIELD: ONE DRINK ★

Scofflaw

The Scofflaw cocktail is also a Prohibition-era classic. The name comes from the term for those individuals that flouted the law and continued to secretly drink spirits in defiance of Prohibition. The drink made its 1924 debut at Harry's New York Bar in Paris, a landmark that was a haven for expatriate Americans and many legendary literary figures and artists. (The Ivories piano bar at Harry's is where George Gershwin composed *An American in Paris*.)

1½ ounces (45 ml) rye whiskey
1 ounce (30 ml) dry vermouth
¾ ounce (22 ml) fresh lemon juice
¾ ounce (22 ml) Homemade Grenadine (page 94)
Garnish: Lemon twist

1. Combine rye, dry vermouth, lemon juice, and grenadine with ice in a shaker and shake until well chilled and incorporated.
2. Strain into a chilled cocktail or coupe glass.
3. Garnish by squeezing the lemon twist over the drink and dropping it in.

★ YIELD: ONE DRINK ★

BLACK CURRANT–KAFFIR LIME "GRENADINE"

Grenadine can also be made from other fruit juices to excellent effect. Black currant or cherry juice works just as well, and the procedure is virtually identical to the standard homemade grenadine recipe (page 94).

1 quart (1 L) black currant juice, divided
6 whole fresh kaffir lime leaves, bruised and shredded
4 cups (950 ml) sugar, divided
½ cup (120 ml) pomegranate molasses
1 teaspoon (5 ml) rosewater (I use Cortas brand)
1 ounce (30 ml) 100 proof vodka

1. Measure 3 cups (710 ml) black currant juice and add to a medium saucepan on the stovetop. Begin heating over medium heat.
2. Add kaffir lime leaves. Bring to a boil, then lower heat to simmer.
3. Add 2½ (595 ml) cups sugar to simmering juice and whisk until dissolved.
4. Continue to simmer until reduced to half the original volume.
5. Add pomegranate molasses and whisk again to incorporate. Simmer gently for 3 more minutes, then remove from heat and allow to cool to room temperature.
6. While the hot-process black currant mixture is reducing, add the remaining sugar to the remaining black currant juice in a large bottle or jar and process, as per cold method, by shaking until all the sugar is completely dissolved.
7. Combine the cooled black currant-kaffir lime mixture with the "cold processed" black currant juice and sugar mixture.
8. Add rosewater and vodka and stir to incorporate.
9. Strain through a fine-mesh strainer to remove any of the kaffir lime leaf debris.
10. Funnel into a clean airtight bottle or container for storage.

★ **YIELD: APPROXIMATELY 5 CUPS (1.2 L)** ★

Properly made, grenadine will be viscous and have a very
sweet, concentrated flavor when it's finished.

Purple Haze

This cocktail's name is a tongue-in-cheek reference to my preferred brand of gin for this cocktail, as well as to the drink's beautiful purple color. I served this drink at a whiskey festival, and after tasting dozens of heavy bourbons and Scotches, most festival-goers relished this drink like they would sorbet at a chili tasting: a delicious palate cleanser.

2 ounces (60 ml) gin (I use Hendrick's)
1 ounce (30 ml) Black Currant–Kaffir Lime Grenadine (page 98)
1 ounce (30 ml) fresh lime juice
½ ounce (15 ml) dry vermouth (I use Dolin)
1½ ounces (45 ml) ginger ale
Garnish: Lime wedge

1. Combine the gin, grenadine, lime juice, and vermouth in a cocktail shaker.
2. Fill with ice, shake, and strain over fresh ice into a Collins glass.
3. Top with the ginger ale.
4. Stir and serve. Garnish with a lime wedge.

★ **YIELD: ONE DRINK** ★

Beautifully and naturally colored, the Purple Hare makes a very crisp, refreshing cocktail.

★ FRESH CITRUS CORDIALS ★

A citrus cordial is a more complex, flavored simple syrup that has been heated to extract all the flavors from the citrus peels. Add a few additional ingredients for depth of flavor, acidity, and shelf stability, and *voilà*! Homemade citrus cordials taste fresher, are easy to prepare, and keep virtually indefinitely if refrigerated. You can now always have your own delicious citrus cordial for gimlets and for creative use as a cocktail ingredient.

{ Rose's Lime Juice Cordial has been produced since the United Kindom's Merchant Shipping Act of 1867 made it compulsory for all ocean-going ships to carry lime-juice rations as a preventative against scurvy. According to author and mixologist Gary Regan, the drink gets its name from the navy surgeon, Sir Thomas D. Gimlette, who encouraged his messmates to take their gin with a healthy dash of lime as a way of preventing scurvy. In his book, *The Bartender's Bible*, Gary Regan also states, ". . . since the Rose's product has such a long and impressive history (which predates the gimlet), I am inclined to think that Rose's was the ingredient that invented the drink." I'm inclined to believe this reverse-engineered theory has some basis in fact. There is a bottle of Rose's lime juice in virtually every bar on the planet. }

RUBY RED GRAPEFRUIT-LEMONGRASS CORDIAL

The idea of creating a grapefruit cordial wasn't a far leap from lime or lemon cordial. This makes a great iteration of a classic cocktail but it can also be used creatively in any recipe calling for grapefruit juice and simple syrup. It's versatile and adds a bit of richness over just straight juice.

3 cups (705 ml) sugar
2 teaspoons (10 ml) citric acid
1 teaspoon (5 ml) tartaric acid (available at homebrew/winemaking supply stores)
2 cups (475 ml) water
2 cups (475 ml) ruby red grapefruit juice
½ cup (120 ml) fresh lemon juice
2 large stalks lemongrass, bruised and finely sliced
Zest of 2 pink grapefruits, removed with a vegetable peeler (to minimize white pith)
1 tablespoon (15 ml) rose flower water
1 teaspoon (5 ml) orange flower water

1. Stir sugar, citric acid, and tartaric acid together with a whisk.
2. Bring the water to a boil and then add the sugar mixture. Stir thoroughly.
3. Juice the "naked" grapefruits and strain juice. Add enough store bought (not from concentrate) ruby red grapefruit juice to equal 2 cups and add to pot.
4. Add lemon juice, lemongrass, and grapefruit zests, and stir. Simmer mixture for 15 to 20 minutes on high heat. Turn off heat, cover, and cool overnight.
5. Strain out and add flower waters. Refrigerate for another day before using (the flavor continues to change a bit). Stored in the refrigerator, it should keep for months.

★ YIELD: ABOUT 6 CUPS (1.5 L) ★

Hemingway Daiquiri

Cordials work really well as a cocktail ingredient, as in this Hemingway Daiquiri—a classic rum cocktail named for Ernest Hemingway, who was apparently quite fond of them.

2½ ounces (70 ml) white rum
1 ounce (28 ml) fresh lime juice
¾ ounce (21 ml) Ruby Red Grapefruit-Lemongrass Cordial (above)
¼ ounce (7 ml) Maraschino liqueur (I like Luxardo brand)
Garnish: Thin lime wheel or pink grapefruit wedge

1. Place all the ingredients in an ice-filled shaker. Shake vigorously, strain into a chilled glass.
2. Garnish with a thin lime wheel floating on the surface or a wedge of pink grapefruit on the rim.

★ YIELD: ONE DRINK ★

LEMON CORDIAL

This Lemon Cordial is fresher and lacking any artificial undertones. Including lemongrass gives this cordial more dimension and a slightly Asian flavor. The Lemon Cordial is used in the Fresh Lemon Gimlet (page 105) and the Front Stoop Lemonade (page 39).

1½ cups (355 ml) sugar
½ tablespoon (7 ml) citric acid
1 teaspoon (5 ml) tartaric acid (available at homebrew/winemaking supply stores)
3 cups (710 ml) water
1½ cups (355 ml) fresh lemon juice and the juice of the four "naked" lemons
Zest of 4 lemons (microplaned)
2 stalks lemongrass, finely chopped
1½ teaspoons (8 ml) orange flower water

1. Combine sugar, citric acid, and tartaric acid in a large bowl (a, b).
2. Stir together with a whisk (c).
3. In a medium-size pot, bring water to a boil, then add the sugar mixture (d).
4. Stir thoroughly to dissolve the sugar mixture into water.

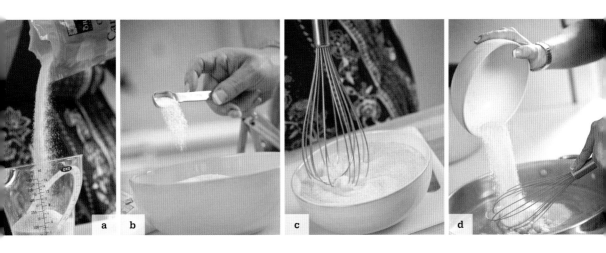

5. Add 1½ cups (355 ml) lemon juice, lemon zest, and lemongrass to the water and sugar mixture and stir (e, f, g, h).
6. Juice the "naked" lemons right into the mixture (i).
7. Cook mixture for 10 minutes over high heat. Turn off the heat, cover with a lid, and cool overnight (j).
8. The next day, strain out the zest and lemongrass pieces and add orange flower water (k, l). Refrigerate for another day before using (the flavor continues to change a bit). Stored in the refrigerator in a sealed glass container, it should keep for up to 4 months.

★ **YIELD: ABOUT 5 CUPS (1.2 L)** ★

Fresh Lemon Gimlet

If a lime gimlet is a classic, a lemon gimlet isn't a far leap for the palate. It has a similar refreshing citrus flavor, but offers a little something for those who don't fancy lime, or might just prefer lemon. Make a pink grapefruit gimlet by substituting grapefruit juice for lemon.

3 ounces (90 ml) gin or vodka
¾ ounce (22 ml) Lemon Cordial (page 103)
Splash of fresh lemon juice
Garnish: Lemon wedge or wheel

1. Shake gin/vodka, Lemon Cordial, and lemon juice over ice until well chilled.
2. Strain into a chilled cocktail or coupe glass to serve straight up, or over fresh ice in a rocks glass to serve on the rocks.
3. Garnish with fresh lemon wedge or wheel.

★ **YIELD: ONE DRINK** ★

The classic counterpart to a lime gimlet, the Fresh Lemon Gimlet is for those who prefer lemon to lime.

FRESH LIME CORDIAL

For this homemade lime cordial, the addition of the kaffir lime leaves creates a richer fresher flavored cordial, that doesn't have that artificial "furniture polish" smell. When removing the peels, it isn't necessary to avoid the white pith, as that adds a desirable slightly bitter note to the final cordial.

1½ cups (355 ml) sugar
½ tablespoon (7 ml) citric acid
1 teaspoon (5 ml) tartaric acid
3 cups (710 ml) water
4 limes, peels removed in thick strips with a
    vegetable peeler or sharp paring knife
1½ cups (355 ml) fresh lime juice + juice
    of the four peeled limes
4 kaffir lime leaves, bruised and shredded
1 teaspoon rosewater

1. Stir sugar, citric acid, and tartaric acid together with a whisk.
2. Bring the water to a boil in a medium saucepan and add sugar mixture. Stir thoroughly to dissolve the sugar mixture into the water.
3. Add lime juice, lime peels, and kaffir lime leaves and stir to combine.
4. Heat mixture for 10 minutes on high heat, turn off heat, cover, and cool overnight.
5. Strain out lime peels and kaffir lime shreds.
6. Add the rosewater and stir to incorporate.
7. Refrigerate for another day before using (the flavor continues to evolve and mellow a bit).
8. Stored in the refrigerator, it should keep almost indefinitely.

★ YIELD: APPROXIMATELY 5 CUPS (1.2 L) ★

Salty Pomeranian

The Salty Pomeranian is a twist on the classic Salty Dog cocktail of vodka and grapefruit juice on the rocks in a salt-rimmed glass. The use of pomegranate vodka helped shape the name.

Kosher salt
2 ounces (60 ml) pomegranate vodka
½ ounce (15 ml) Fresh Lime Cordial
½ ounce (15 ml) fresh lime juice
½ ounce (15 ml) Simple Syrup (page 34)
2 ounces (60 ml) ruby red grapefruit juice
Garnish: Lime wedge

1. Wipe the edge of a tall collins glass with the lime wedge, then dip the rim in kosher salt.
2. Pack the glass with ice.
3. Shake all ingredients over ice and pour carefully into the salt-rimmed collins glass.
4. Garnish with a lime wedge.

★ **YIELD: ONE DRINK** ★

Salty Pomeranian Variation:

The Salty Pomeranian is also delicious if you substitute 2 ounces (60 ml) gin for the pomegranate vodka, cut the fresh lime juice and simple syrup down to ¼ ounce (7 ml) each, and add ½ ounce (15 ml) of pomegranate juice to the recipe.

Fresh Lime Gimlet

Everyone loves a gimlet: bracing sweet-tart lime flavor combined with ice-cold gin or vodka. What's not to love? And now that you have a cordial recipe, you can have your classic Gimlet in any flavor you've created.

3 ounces (90 ml) gin or vodka
¾ ounce (22 ml) Fresh Lime Cordial (page 106)
Splash of fresh lime juice
Garnish: Lime wedge

1. Shake gin/vodka, lime cordial, and lime juice over ice until well chilled.
2. Strain into a chilled cocktail or coupe glass to serve straight up, or over fresh ice in a rocks glass to serve on the rocks.
3. Garnish with fresh lime wedge.

★ **YIELD: ONE DRINK** ★

Ginger beer became popular in England in the mid-eighteenth century. It was fermented and brewed from ginger, sugar, water, and yeast. It reached its peak of popularity in the early twentieth century, by which time it had made its way to the United States and Canada. It's the key ingredient in a Moscow Mule, the famed cocktail from the vodka craze of the 1950s. Nowadays, ginger beer is almost always produced as a nonalcoholic soft drink, and there are several brands available commercially.

HOMEMADE GINGER BEER CONCENTRATE

This version is my own adaptation of mixologist Audrey Saunders's ginger beer recipe from her stellar cocktail lounge, the Pegu Club in SoHo, New York City. This recipe has a high yield, but it is very easy to halve it for a smaller batch.

1 gallon (3.8 L) water
1 pound (½ kg) ginger root, dark spots removed and sliced into coins (a)
½ cup (120 ml) fresh lime juice
½ cup of light brown sugar

1. In a large pot, bring the water to a boil. While you are waiting for water to boil, place sliced ginger into the blender container (b).
2. Add approximately 2 cups (475 ml) of hot water from the gallon that is heating (this makes processing the ginger easier) (c).
3. Process until ginger is a mulch-like puree (d).

a

b

c

d

Nonalcoholic ginger beer is delicious and refreshing as is, or used as a cocktail ingredient.

4. Wait for the water to come to a full boil and pour the ginger puree back into the hot water (e).
5. Simmer for approximately 5 minutes.
6. Remove from heat, cover, and let stand for 1 hour. Add the lime juice and the light brown sugar, and stir well to dissolve (f).
7. Allow to cool for several hours or overnight. There will be a great deal of sediment at the bottom of the container. This is normal.
8. Strain the liquid through a fine strainer or a chinoise. The strongest part of the ginger essence is still in the solids, and needs to be pressed out manually. Press down on the solids with a spoon, ladle, or potato masher to remove all of the liquid and flavor from the solids (g). This is a very important step in order to extract all the flavor. Its appearance after straining will be cloudy.
9. Funnel into clean containers. It can be stored for up to 2 weeks (in the refrigerator), but try to use when fresh, as the strength of the ginger fades over time, and the ginger beer will eventually start to ferment. Ginger sediment will sink to the bottom of the container, which is completely normal. Shake before using. If you want to keep this longer, it can be divided into plastic quart containers and frozen immediately. If it is frozen right away, it will still be fresh and spicy when it is defrosted.
10. To serve, mix with an equal part of regular or diet ginger ale to dilute the very strong spicy flavor and to slightly carbonate it. This can be served as is for a deliciously refreshing and spicy nonalcoholic soft drink or used as an ingredient in cocktails.

★ **YIELD: 1 GALLON (3.8 L)** ★

Dark 'n' Stormy

In Bermuda, the Dark 'n' Stormy is a registered trademark of Gosling's Brothers Limited, and is described as Bermuda's national drink. It is one of the few cocktails known to have an actual trademark. Legend has it that the cocktail was named for its resemblance to the murky skies preceding a bad storm that only a fool would dare to sail.

2 ounces (60 ml) rum (use Gosling's, for authenticity)
3 ounces (90 ml) Homemade Ginger Beer Concentrate (remember to shake before using) (page 109)
3 ounces (90 ml) regular or diet ginger ale
Squeeze of fresh lime juice
Garnish: Lime wedge

1. Pour rum, Homemade Ginger Beer Concentrate, ginger ale, and fresh lime juice into an ice-filled collins glass.
2. Stir gently to combine thoroughly.
3. Garnish with a lime wedge.

★ **YIELD: ONE DRINK** ★

Gin-Gin Mule (courtesy of Audrey Saunders)

This modern classic cocktail combines herbaceous mint with lime and ginger beer and makes for one truly refreshing drink on a hot summer day. Think of it as a gin and ginger mojito—and enjoy!

¾ ounce (22 ml) fresh lime juice
1 ounce (30 ml) Simple Syrup (page 34)
1 mint sprig (for muddling)
1 ounce (30 ml) Homemade Ginger Beer Concentrate (page 109)
1¾ (52 ml) ounces gin (Audrey prefers Tanqueray)
Garnish: Mint sprig, lime wheel, candied ginger.

1. Measure lime juice, Simple Syrup, and mint into a mixing glass. Muddle well.
2. Add ginger beer, gin, and ice.
3. Shake well, and strain over fresh ice into a highball glass.
4. Garnish with mint sprig, lime wheel, and ginger, and serve with long straws.

If you have Mint Syrup on hand (see page 40), you can substitute 1 ounce (30 ml) of Mint Syrup and skip the muddling step.

★ **YIELD: ONE DRINK** ★

Pink Sapphire Swizzle

The Angostura bitters, Thai basil sprig, and orange oils are a big nose full of aromatics as you bring the glass to your lips.

2 ounces (60 ml) gin (I use Bombay Sapphire)
½ ounce (15 ml) Thai Basil Syrup (page 38)
½ ounce (15 ml) Homemade Ginger Beer Concentrate (page 109)
¾ ounce (22 ml) Falernum (either homemade, page 117, or Taylor's Velvet Falernum)
¾ ounce (22 ml) fresh lime juice
2 dashes orange bitters
2 dashes Angostura bitters
½ ounce (15 ml) pomegranate juice
Garnish: 4 dashes Angostura bitters, sprig of Thai basil, fat twist of orange peel

1. Pack a tall glass with crushed ice.
2. Add gin, Thai Basil Syrup, ginger beer, Falernum, lime juice, orange bitters, Angostura bitters, and pomegranate juice.
3. Swizzle with bar spoon or swizzle stick until outside of glass is frozen and frosty, and drink is thoroughly combined.
4. Top with more crushed ice.
5. Garnish with a float of the Angostura bitters, a spanked sprig of Thai basil, and spray the surface of the drink with orange oils from the orange zest.
6. Drink with a straw.

★ **YIELD: ONE DRINK** ★

The following recipes are staples of classic bars. They have completely unique flavors and endless flavor combinations. Enjoy!

ORGEAT SYRUP

Orgeat (OAR-zhott) is a much under-appreciated cocktail flavoring. Once an essential ingredient in tiki drinks, it seems to have fallen out of fashion. The word orgeat is derived from the Latin root *hordeata*, or "made with barley," which was how orgeat was originally derived. For those familiar with Mexican *agua fresca* drinks, *horchata*, or almond water, has the same origin. Orgeat is the defining ingredient in the Mai Tai and is also used in several other classic drinks, including the Japanese Cocktail. Although commercial versions of orgeat are readily available, making your own is fairly straightforward and yields a far more fresh and flavorful result. Orgeat would be a great gift for your cocktail-enthusiast friends. Make a big batch and pour it into attractive bottles with a recipe for a Mai Tai tied around the neck of each bottle.

Making orgeat often involves several days of multiple soakings and straining of peeled and chopped almonds in water to extract the oils and flavor. I've created a shorter process here that yields excellent results overnight, with only one soak and straining required. I add a small amount of organic almond extract to provide the slightly bitter almond flavor commercial orgeat syrups possess, because they are made with bitter almonds that aren't readily available to the home cook due to the presence of cyanide in them. Although cooking bitter almonds will neutralize the toxic effects of the small amount of cyanide present, bitter almonds are restricted and difficult to procure. The small amount of almond extract will replace that marzipan-like flavor that won't come from the almond oils of sweet almonds alone.

With the small amount of almond peel that might be present on the almonds, this orgeat can be a bit more "beige" than the pristine milky white of commercial orgeat syrups, but it has no ill effect on the flavor in cocktails. Some details just aren't worth sweating over. If it tastes good and looks great in the glass, that's all that matters. If you wish, you may use blanched and peeled slivered or sliced almonds to achieve a clearer result.

16 ounces (453 g) raw sliced almonds
2 ounces (60 ml) overproof vodka
5 cups (1.2 L) hot filtered water
4½ cups (1 L) sugar
⅓ cup (80 ml) brandy or cognac
1 teaspoon (5 ml) rosewater
1½ teaspoons (8 ml) orange flower water
½ teaspoon (3 ml) organic almond extract
¼ teaspoon xanthan gum

1. Preheat oven to 350°F (177° C). Spread almonds in a thin layer on a nonstick cookie sheet (a).
2. Roast the almonds in 2-minute intervals (set a timer to remind yourself!) for a total of 8 minutes, stirring every 2 minutes to keep from browning. The goal is not to toast them, but to "loosen" up the oils they contain, so they'll extract more easily.
3. Remove the almonds from the oven immediately and pour the hot almonds into the blender container so they do not continue to brown on the hot cookie sheet. The almonds should only be very lightly toasted around the edges, if at all (b).
4. Pour the 2 ounces (60 ml) of vodka over the hot almonds and steep for 10 minutes.
5. Add 5 cups (1.2 L) of hot filtered water to blender container (c) and pulse until the almonds are chopped into small bits, about the size of peanut bits in chunky peanut butter (d).
6. Soak the almond bits overnight.
7. The next day, strain the almond bits and liquid in small batches through a cheesecloth-lined fine-mesh strainer into a bowl, squeezing the almond bits in the cheesecloth to extract all of the oils and flavor (e). Don't be afraid to really wring this out hard. You need to get out the almonds' oils so your orgeat will taste strongly of almond (f).
8. Measure the liquid; there should be approximately 4½ cups (1 L).

a

b

c

d

e

f

9. Gently heat the almond liquid in a saucepan (g).
10. Add the sugar and stir until it is dissolved. Remove from heat immediately. Allow almond syrup to cool slightly.
11. Add the brandy, the rosewater, the orange flower water, and the almond extract (h). Stir vigorously to incorporate all the ingredients you've just added.
12. Add a small amount of the mixed orgeat to xanthan gum in a small cup. Stir or whisk gently to incorporate without any lumps. Add xanthan gum slurry back into the full batch of orgeat and stir to combine thoroughly.
13. Funnel into clean glass bottles for storage. This syrup keeps refrigerated for several months.

★ YIELD: APPROXIMATELY 6 CUPS (1.4 L) ★

{ Note: Orgeat is an emulsion; even though the xanthan gum will stabilize it a bit, the oils and water will separate over time into a milky layer and a syrup layer. Always shake thoroughly before using. }

Mai Tai

The Mai Tai is the quintessential tiki cocktail. As with many recipe rivalries, there are various stories circulating about its origins. Some credit Victor Bergeron of Oakland's Trader Vic's with creating it in 1944. Don the Beachcomber takes credit for creating the drink with a slightly different recipe in 1933. Both versions are delicious. The following recipe is my own spin. The float of dark rum on the top adds an aromatic note and changes its character by mixing in while you drink it.

1 ounce (30 ml) light rum
1 ounce (30) ml) dark rum
1 ounce (30 ml) fresh lime juice
¾ ounce (22 ml) Orgeat Syrup (page 114)
½ ounce (15 ml) orange Curaçao (I prefer Cointreau or Luxardo Triplum)
Optional: ½ ounce (15 ml) float of dark rum
Garnish: Mint sprig, cocktail cherry, and lime wedge

1. Shake all the ingredients in a shaker with ice, and strain into a rocks glass over crushed ice.
2. If desired, slowly pour dark rum over surface of drink to create a "float" on the surface.
3. Garnish with fruits and mint, and serve with a straw.

★ YIELD: ONE DRINK ★

FALERNUM

Falernum (fuh-LEARN-um) is a rum-based simple syrup flavored with almond, ginger, cloves, and lime. There's no true substitute as the flavor is quite unique. This falernum recipe is from my friend and colleague, Maria Polise.

10 ounces (300 ml) overproof (126 proof) rum (Wray & Nephew preferred)
2 ounces (60 ml) 151 proof Demerara rum (Lemon Hart preferred)
Zest of 12 limes
3 ounces (85 g) roughly chopped fresh ginger
4 large chunks cinnamon bark
10 cracked French roast coffee beans
40 cloves
20 cracked allspice berries
6 ounces (180 ml) fresh lime juice
3 cups (710 ml) Demerara Simple Syrup (page 34)
1 teaspoon (5 ml) organic almond extract
¾ ounce (22 ml) Angostura bitters

1. Pour the rums into an airtight container. Add lime zest, ginger, cinnamon bark, coffee beans, cloves, and allspice berries and soak for 48 hours.
2. Strain, and add lime juice, Demerara Simple Syrup, almond extract, and Angostura bitters.
3. Shake to combine all ingredients. This syrup keeps refrigerated almost indefinitely due to the high level of alcohol.

★ **YIELD: APPROXIMATELY 5 CUPS (1.2 L)** ★

Rhum Ricardo (courtesy of Maria Polise)

This recipe is Maria's expanded version of a rum rickey.

¼ ounce (7 ml) absinthe
2 ounces (60 ml) white rhum agricole (such as Rhum Clement Premier Canne)
¾ ounce (22 ml) lime juice
½ ounce (15 ml) Falernum (above)
½ ounce (15 ml) agave nectar
Club soda
Garnish: Lime wheel

1. Rinse a collins glass with absinthe and fill with ice.
2. Shake rhum, lime juice, falernum, and agave nectar over ice in a cocktail shaker. Strain into the ice-filled collins glass, top with soda, stir, and garnish with a lime wheel.

★ **YIELD: ONE DRINK** ★

PIMENTO (OR ALLSPICE) DRAM

Pimiento or pimento dram is a mysterious and misunderstood Caribbean cocktail ingredient that few had ever heard of prior to the cocktail resurgence. But like falernum, it is both essential to certain cocktails and adds an irreplaceable flavor component to the cocktails in which it is featured. Pimento is native to Jamaica and is the berry from which allspice is derived. English explorers coined the name *allspice* because the berries seemed to incorporate the familiar dessert spice flavors of cinnamon, nutmeg, and clove all at once. While once very difficult to procure, there are a few brands of commercially available pimento drams on the market, such as St. Elizabeth Allspice Dram and Bitter Truth Pimento Dram. Making your own pimento dram saves the bother of tracking down the elusive spirit.

This recipe requires a bit of advanced planning because the steeping and resting process takes about 8 weeks. Your patience will be rewarded when you have a batch of this delicious spirit to enjoy in some of the following cocktails.

2 cups (475 ml) overproof rum (such as Wray & Nephew)
¾ cup allspice berries
6 black peppercorns
6 cloves
2 cinnamon sticks, crushed
1 nutmeg, crushed with a mallet into small (rice-size) chunks
1 piece (1 inch or 2.5 cm) of vanilla bean, split open
1 cup (235 ml) dark rum (such as Myers)
3 cups (710 ml) water
3½ cups (830 ml) Demerara sugar
½ ounce (15 ml) Angostura bitters

1. Place the overproof rum in a large airtight jar.
2. Mix allspice berries, peppercorns, and cloves and grind coarsely in a coffee grinder or in a mortar.
3. Add the crushed spices—cinnamon, nutmeg, and vanilla bean—to rum in the jar, and allow mixture to steep for 2 weeks, agitating the jar daily.
4. Add the dark rum and steep for 1 more week.
5. At the end of 3 weeks, pour the mixture through a chinoise or a cheesecloth-lined fine strainer, pressing on the solids to extract as much of the spiced rum as you can. Pour the liquid again through a coffee filter, removing any powdery residue and small bits of spices.
6. Make a syrup with the sugar and water, placing over gentle heat and stirring the mixture until the sugar is completely dissolved.
7. Let the syrup cool, then add it to the infused rum along with the Angostura bitters.
8. Bottle the mixture in two clean/sterilized 750 ml bottles and let it rest for 1 month while the flavors mellow and blend together.

★ YIELD: APPROXIMATELY TWO 750-ML BOTTLES ★

Lion's Tail

The Lion's Tail is one of the better known cocktails using Pimento Dram. It has a predominant flavor of bourbon but is balanced by the sweetness and spiciness from the dram and the acidity of the lime. It is an excellent cocktail for cooler weather.

2 ounces (60 ml) bourbon
½ ounce (15 ml) fresh lime juice
¼ ounce (7 ml) Pimento Dram (opposite)
¼ ounce (7 ml) Demerara Simple Syrup (page 34)
1 dash Angostura Bitters

1. Add bourbon, lime juice, Pimento Dram, and Demerara Simple Syrup to a shaker tin and top with ice.
2. Shake vigorously until well chilled, and strain into a chilled cocktail/coupe glass.

★ **YIELD: ONE DRINK** ★

None But the Brave

Surprisingly smooth, the spice of the dram and the dark rum are a delicious combo. The brandy provides a warming base and the lemon juice gives the drink more balance, and keeps it from being too sweet. The cocktail is named after either a line from a 1697 John Dryden poem ("None but the brave deserve the fair…") or a 1965 Frank Sinatra movie titled the same. Since the first written mention of this drink is in the 1941 first edition of Crosby Gaige's *Cocktail Guide and Ladies' Companion*, it would seem that Dryden can claim credit for naming both the cocktail *and* the film.

1½ ounces (45 ml) cognac
½ ounce (15 ml) Pimento Dram
¼ ounce (7 ml) fresh lemon luice
¼ ounce (7 ml) dark rum
¼ teaspoon (1 ml) Simple Syrup (page 34)

1. Add cognac, Pimento Dram, lemon juice, rum, and Simple Syrup to an ice-filled shaker.
2. Shake vigorously to thoroughly combine ingredients.
3. Strain into a chilled cocktail or coupe glass.

★ **YIELD: ONE DRINK** ★

TRUFFLE-HONEY SYRUP

1 quart (3.8 L) water
2 cups (400 g) sugar
2 tablespoons black truffle honey, or 3 tablespoons white truffle honey

1. Bring ingredients to a boil for 15 minutes.
2. Let cool in refrigerator for 12 hours.

★ YIELD: ONE QUART (1 L) ★

Versailles (courtesy of Ryan Reigel)

The idea of putting cheese, especially a highly pungent one like blue cheese, into a cocktail may seem somewhat *off*-putting at first glance. However, the earthy savoriness of truffle, the saltiness of the cheese, and the natural sweetness of rum, blueberries, and honey just work together somehow in this innovative cocktail that is featured in the beautiful bar at the Ritz Carlton, Philadelphia.

8-10 Blueberries
1¼ ounces (37 ml) rum (preferably 10 Cane)
½ ounce (15 ml) Truffle-Honey Syrup
¾ ounce (22 ml) fresh lemon juice
Lemon-lime soda
Garnish: blue cheese, about the size of an acorn

1. Muddle the blueberries. Add remaining ingredients and shake with ice.
2. Pour over fresh ice into a highball glass and top with lemon-lime soda.
3. Garnish with a blue cheese, preferably Danish or another soft blue cheese. Stir gently to allow cheese to melt into drink.

★ YIELD: ONE DRINK ★

BASIC BLOODY MARY MIX

Bloody Mary mix has as many variations as there are bartenders mixing it. Everyone has an opinion on what kind of hot sauce to use, whether or not to use horseradish, what to utilize as the salt in the recipe, tomato juice or blended vegetable juice, and so on. This is one very forgiving recipe, so you may change this to suit your own taste.

1 46-ounce (1.3 L) can or bottle of vegetable juice, such as V-8 (or regular tomato juice)
3 tablespoons (45 g) prepared horseradish
1 tablespoon (11 g) spicy Creole mustard
2 tablespoons (10 ml) Worcestershire sauce
¼ cup (60 ml) fresh lemon juice
2 tablespoons (30 ml) Tabasco sauce
½ tablespoon (9 g) celery salt
½ tablespoon (9 g) salt and each freshly ground black pepper

Mix all the ingredients together in a large container and whisk vigorously to combine, or blend by pulsing gently in the blender. This keeps very well when refrigerated, however the spices and horseradish will separate and fall to the bottom. Be certain to shake thoroughly before using.

★ YIELD: ABOUT 5 CUPS (1.2 L) ★

Smokin' Mary (or Smokin' Snapper or Maria)

2 ounces (60 ml) vodka (or gin, or tequila)
4 ounces Basic Bloody Mary Mix (above)
3 whole carrots, peeled and cut into thin matchsticks
   approximately 4˝ (10 cm) in length
4 whole poblano peppers, halved and seeded
3 celery stalks, peeled to remove outer fibers and cut into 4˝ (10 cm) lengths

1. Prepare wood chips and smoker according to manufacturer's directions.
   Smoke carrots, peppers, and celery approximately 20–25 minutes until softened.
2. Turn off the heat source. Allow vegetables to cool inside smoker for at least 30 minutes.
3. Add to blender with Basic Bloody Mary Mix and puree thoroughly.
4. For each cocktail, add 2 ounces vodka to shaker and fill with 4 ounces Smokin' Mary mix.
5. Shake and strain over fresh ice.

★ YIELD: ONE DRINK ★

NOTE: To prepare Smokin' Mary by the pitcher for brunch parties choose a base spirit and add twice the volume of mix. Stir well to incorporate and serve in tall glasses over ice. Garnish with citrus wedges, celery sticks, olives, pickled okra, or beef jerky strips as a stirrer.

★ YIELD: 8-10 DRINKS ★

The following recipes for cocktail cherries and cocktail onions are the perfect way to elevate your homemade cocktails into something even more special.

COCKTAIL ONIONS

Cocktail onions are one of those strange bar condiments that no one seems to care deeply about, or know what to do with. But a really well-made cocktail onion is a beautiful thing. They make a great garnish for a Bloody Mary or are tasty on a relish tray along with pickles and green tomatoes. There are plenty of ways to enjoy a fine pickled onion. And once you taste these, I'm certain you can come up with plenty of your own ideas.

2 pounds (910 g) pearl onions (I like a mix of half white and half red pearl onions)
1 quart (1 L) champagne vinegar
3 cups (710 ml) warm filtered water
2 cups (400 g) granulated sugar
2 tablespoons (38 g) kosher salt
2 teaspoons (7 g) mustard seeds
2 teaspoons (3 g) whole allspice
1 teaspoon (2 g) coriander seeds
1 teaspoon (2 g) whole cloves
½ teaspoon (1 g) ground ginger
½ teaspoon (0.5 g) dried red pepper flakes
2 bay leaves, crumbled
2-inch (5-cm) piece cinnamon stick
½ cup (120 ml) dry vermouth

1. Peel the pearl onions by cutting a small X-shaped mark in the stem end of the onions and blanching them in boiling water for 1 minute. Drain and place into a bowl of ice water, and the skins should slip off easily. Transfer onions to a clean glass jar.
2. Combine vinegar, warm water, sugar, and salt. Stir until completely dissolved.
3. Tie pickling spices into a square of cheesecloth and place in the champagne vinegar solution. Bring to a boil and lower heat. Simmer spice sachet for about 5 minutes.
4. Remove from heat and cool slightly. Remove spice sachet. Pour just enough pickling liquid over the onions to cover. Allow to cool overnight, covered, at room temperature.
5. Add vermouth and shake to incorporate.

Keep the onions refrigerated for up to 3 months.

★ YIELD: APPROXIMATELY 1½ PINTS (710 ML) ★

Gibson

The Gibson is a tasty alternative to the standard olive- or twist-garnished martini, and is good when you're feeling in the mood for something a little different. Adding homemade cocktail onions elevates this drink to *unique*.

2½ ounces (75 ml) gin
½ ounce (15 ml) dry vermouth (I prefer Dolin)
Garnish: 1 or 3 cocktail onions*

1. Pour the ingredients into a mixing glass with ice cubes. Stir well.
2. Strain into chilled cocktail/coupe glass.
3. Garnish with the cocktail onion(s).

*In some circles, an even number of olives or onions to garnish your cocktail is considered bad luck. I think that odd numbers just look more visually pleasing.

★ **YIELD: ONE DRINK** ★

COCKTAIL CHERRIES

I have feelings of genuine loathing toward packaged commercial maraschino cherries. They're bleached, re-dyed to a color not found in nature with artificial, possibly carcinogenic, chemicals and doused with artificial flavorings. They're an abomination that should never pollute a lovingly crafted cocktail. Fortunately, making your own cocktail cherries is pretty simple, and the end result is far tastier and more aesthetically pleasing in your cocktails. Problem solved.

3 cups (710) water
1 teaspoon (5 g) salt
1½ pounds (680 g) stem on ripe cherries, rinsed and pitted
2 cups (400 g) sugar
6 cloves
1 star anise
1 cinnamon stick
15 cherry pits
½ teaspoon lemon zest
½ cup (120 ml) brandy or cognac
½ cup (120 ml) cherry liqueur (I use Cherry Heering)
½ teaspoon (2 ml) organic vanilla extract

1. Bring the water to a boil in a large shallow saucepan. Add salt.
2. Add the cherries, reduce the heat and blanch for 2 minutes (a).
3. Strain out cherries, reserving poaching liquid (b).
4. Place cherries in an ice-water bath to stop them from cooking and getting too soft. Strain again and place cherries into a clean, airtight jar (c).
5. Measure out two cups (475 ml) of the cherry poaching liquid and return to saucepan. Begin heating over medium heat. Add the sugar and stir to dissolve. Add spices, cherry pits, and lemon zest and bring to a boil. Boil gently for 5 minutes (d).
6. Remove from heat and cool for 1 hour.
7. Add brandy, cherry liqueur, and vanilla extract to spiced cherry syrup.
8. Strain the spiced and spiked syrup over the cherries in the jar (e).
9. Let the cherries age for at least 2 weeks before using.

The cherries will soften and take on the flavors of the spices and spirits as they age. When the cherries are done, they will keep almost indefinitely refrigerated, as long as the liquid in the jar covers the cherries. If the cherries are exposed to air, they will begin to grow mold. Cocktail cherries are the perfect garnish for your Manhattans or are delicious muddled into an Old Fashioned.

★ **YIELD: APPROXIMATELY 1½ PINTS (710 ML)** ★

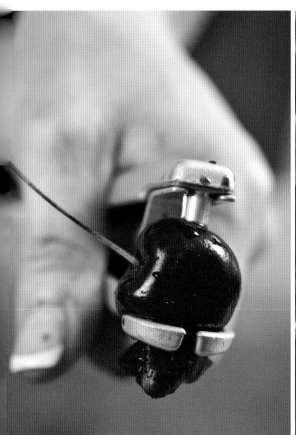

Removing the pits make the cherries easier to eat without breaking a tooth and opens up the fruit to absorb more flavor from your preserving liquid.

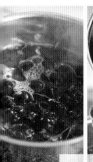

Money Manhattan

The Manhattan is in the pantheon of classic cocktails, and it is one of the six basic drinks listed in David Embury's 1948 classic *The Fine Art of Mixing Drinks*. There are plenty of stories about its origins, including one that credits Lady Randolph Churchill, mother of Winston Churchill, for its creation, but the timing of that story makes it suspect. Its exact origins are hazy.

A Manhattan has three basic ingredients: whiskey, sweet vermouth, and bitters. By elevating the quality of each of those ingredients, and using the best whiskey and vermouth you can find plus homemade cocktail cherries, the end result is greater than the sum of its parts. The name of this cocktail comes from a customer declaring "That's money!" the first time I made one for him.

2½ ounces (75 ml) bourbon or rye
¾ ounce (22 ml) Carpano Antica vermouth
1 bar spoon of cherry juice from Cocktail Cherries (page 124)
2 dashes Angostura bitters
4–5 drops Fee Brothers whiskey barrel–aged bitters
Garnish: Homemade cocktail cherry (page 124)

1. Pour the ingredients into a mixing glass with ice cubes. Stir until well chilled.
2. Strain into chilled cocktail/coupe glass to serve straight up, or over fresh ice in a rocks glass to serve on the rocks.
3. Garnish with the cocktail cherry.

{ Fee Brothers whiskey barrel–aged bitters have a very distinctive Christmas potpourri scent and dessert-spice flavor to them. There's nothing else quite like them. A little bit goes a very long way. I keep these in an eye dropper so I can dole them out in a controlled fashion. }

★ YIELD: ONE DRINK ★

CHAPTER 4

INFUSIONS

Besides cooking up your own bar mixers, there's a whole other world of creativity to be explored in making your own infusions. Have you ever been to a bar and seen large glass jars filled with fruit and liquid? Those are the house-made infusions at work. Infusing is the process of extracting flavors from fruits, herbs, and/or spices by steeping or soaking in alcohol, and you can easily make these at home.

Until recently, there were still Prohibition-era laws on the books banning these very drinks. And after several bartenders were fined for serving infused liquors and a few restaurants were forced to either dump gallons of liquor or have it confiscated by the authorities, a grassroots campaign was started by a few artisan cocktail bartenders, and the case was argued and won. It seems that good infusions are worth fighting for and legislating!

I've been an "infusionista" for several years now, and infusions can be created for just about any drink imaginable. You can make flavored spirits to mix into your favorite cocktails or to sip straight or on the rocks. The possibilities are virtually limitless, and the only thing required is the knowledge of what flavor combinations you enjoy, access to excellent ingredients, and a little bit of patience.

Think of the flavor combinations in your favorite cocktails and take that as a jumping off point for your creativity.

★ Vodka is the most commonly infused spirit, because it's the tofu of the spirit world—it's virtually tasteless and will take on whatever flavors you pair it with. Any spirit can be infused, and the aromatics and flavor structure of the base spirit will help you choose complementary flavors.

★ The botanical aspects of gin make infusing it with citrus or cucumber very appealing.

★ Rum's natural sweetness makes an excellent base for tropical fruit or tea infusions.

★ The earthiness of tequila pairs well with sweet berry flavors.

»» Base Spirits ««

The base spirit will set the foundation for a good infusion. Choosing a decent quality spirit that is smooth and clean will allow the added flavors to be the star, but it isn't necessary to spend a fortune on the base spirit. The subtleties of top-shelf spirits are lost when they're masked by the infused flavors.

If you're experimenting with a new flavor combination or one that isn't coming directly from a pretested recipe, you may want to use a less expensive bottle so as not to waste money or good liquor. Or simply make a very small test batch. Sometimes those ideas that work in your head don't work out so well in practice.

»» Choosing Your Ingredients ««

Fruits, vegetables, fresh herbs, spices, and combinations of those elements are most commonly used for infusions. The most popular infusions are fruit based. Pineapple, mango, and melon are popular vodka infusions.

Mixing fruit with a complementary herb or spice is an easy equation for creating a simple but delicious infusion. Lemon-rosemary, ginger-mint, watermelon-basil, cucumber-dill, apple-cinnamon, or any other combination that you love can be made in a few short days. For best results, use fresh seasonal produce and dried spices that you know are sourced from a reliable purveyor that has high turnover so their products are always fragrant and fresh.

»» How to Make Infusions ««

★ The infusion process itself is quite straightforward. What you're trying to accomplish is to use the ethanol in your base spirit as a solvent to strip the volatile oils and flavors from your flavoring agents. Ethanol is pure 200-proof (100%) alcohol. By using a base spirit with a proof level of 80–150 proof (40–75% alcohol by volume), the ethanol is able to dissolve those substances that are less soluble in water, while at the same time the water content can dissolve the substances less soluble in ethanol. Since ethanol has an almost neutral pH level, it works well dissolving either alkaline or acidic botanical components while maintaining a balanced end result.

★ Choose a clean airtight jar in which to make your infusion. Quart (liter)-sized mason jars work well, or if you're making a larger batch, a cleaned commercial gallon (4-liter) jar from a restaurant or bar works well. If you're experimenting and want to create small batches of a variety of flavors at once, using smaller canning jars will allow you to divide your bottle of spirit into a few jars.

★ Wash the ingredients, cut your fruits, pick over your spices or bruise your fresh herbs, and place them inside the jar. Fill the jar with your spirit, cover tightly with a lid, and shake a few times.

»» Storing the Infusion ««

Most infusion recipes suggest storing your infusions in a cool, dark place and shaking or stirring it 3 to 5 times a day for the duration of the infusion. I prefer to refrigerate infusions that contain ingredients that would spoil at room temperature (like cut fresh fruits or vegetables), just to be on the safe side and avoid any possibility of food-borne illnesses. Dried spices and fresh herbs can be kept without refrigeration. On average, the ingredients should stay in the liquor for 3 to 5 days. More intense flavors (e.g. fresh horseradish root, habanero peppers) may only need 3 days, less intense flavors (apples, fresh berries, dried spices) should stay in the jar for a full week or more. You will want to taste test your creation every few days to see if the flavors have adequately transferred and are balanced to your taste.

»» Straining the Infusion ««

Once the infusion has reached its peak in flavor, you need to remove the flavoring ingredients from the jar. Use a fine strainer, cheesecloth, chinoise, or gold coffee filter to strain the infused spirit into another clean jar or bowl. If you plan to store it in the infusion jar, wash out the jar before returning the infused spirits. Or you can funnel the infusion into a clean bottle for storage. I follow the same rules for storage that I do for refrigerating the infusions while they're in process. If it contains any ingredients that you wouldn't normally leave out on the counter or in a cabinet unrefrigerated, then refrigerate the finished infusion. If there's nothing in the infusion that might spoil, then store the finished infusion as you would any other liquor of its type. While the alcohol content will inhibit bacterial growth, and the infusion has been strained, there is no guarantee that any trace amounts of organic ingredients that might linger in the final infusion might not go bad. Better to be safe than to risk an unpleasant case of food poisoning, even if that risk is remote.

Vodka and gin are very versatile and I've showcased that here with the many varied flavor profiles. Some work great with other alcohols as well. Experiment with some of my suggestions.

PINEAPPLE VODKA

This is one of the easiest infusions to create. Stacking up the pineapple slices like bricks around the perimeter of the infusion jar makes for a beautiful display while the fruit is infusing. This recipe works perfectly with rum or tequila as well, and those infusions can be enjoyed simply chilled or as an ingredient in your favorite rum drink or margarita.

2 large pineapples
1 bottle (1.75-liter) vodka

1. Remove the top leaves from the pineapples. Peel the pineapples and quarter them lengthwise.
2. Slice off the tough inner core from each pineapple quarter. Slice quarters into ¼" (6 mm) -thick slices.
3. Stack slices alternating like bricks around the perimeter of the inside of your infusion jar, leaving the center space open.
4. When the jar is filled with all the slices, pour the vodka gently into the center space, filling up the jar and spaces between the fruit slices.
5. IMPORTANT: Cover all of the fruit completely with vodka and do not leave any fruit exposed to air at the top of the jar as a way to discourage any mold growth.

For maximum flavor, infuse pineapples in the vodka for 10 days out of direct sunlight. Strain off the vodka, and funnel it into clean bottles for storage. Keep it refrigerated. The fruit can be eaten, but a lot of the flavor will have leeched into the vodka.

★ **YIELD: APPROXIMATELY 1.75 LITERS** ★

Steakhouse Pineapple Martini

This is the easiest cocktail in the world once you've had the patience to make the infused vodka. In addition to drinking it simply chilled, this vodka makes an excellent ingredient for tiki-style cocktails.

3 ounces (90 ml) Pineapple Vodka (opposite)
Garnish: Pineapple slice or lime wedge

1. Pour the vodka into an ice-filled shaker.
2. Shake until well chilled and strain into a chilled cocktail glass or coupe.
3. Garnish with a pineapple slice or lime wedge if desired.

★ **YIELD: ONE DRINK** ★

CUCUMBER VODKA/GIN

Because of the high water content, cucumber infuses fairly quickly and the flavor works well with either vodka or gin. It makes for a cool and refreshing summer cocktail on ice, served with soda or tonic water or mixed into a gimlet or martini. Even "seedless" cucumbers should have the center sections removed to avoid any bitter flavors that might be imparted by the small seeds that are still present.

1 large cucumber, preferably English or hothouse "seedless" cucumber, peeled
1 bottle (750-ml) bottle vodka or gin

1. Slice peeled cucumber lengthwise. Seed the cucumbers by running a teaspoon gently down the center and removing any small seeds and spongy center parts. Slice the seeded cucumber halves into thin half moons and place in a clean infusion jar.
2. Cover the slices with vodka or gin. Steep for 3 to 5 days out of direct sunlight in a cool place. Do not steep for any longer than this, or the spirit will begin to take on a bitter flavor, even with the seeds removed.
3. Strain out cucumber slices and discard them. Funnel into clean bottles for storage. Keep refrigerated.

★ **YIELD: 750 ML** ★

Cucumber Gimlet

You can make cucumber gimlets with commercially available flavored vodkas, but making these yourself is easy and tastes much more fresh and natural. The combination of cucumber and lime is very refreshing!

3 ounces (90 ml) Cucumber Vodka or Gin (page 133)
¾ ounce (22 ml) ounce Fresh Lime Cordial (page 106)
Splash of fresh lime juice
Garnish: Cucumber wheel and lime twist

1. Shake Cucumber Vodka/Gin, Fresh Lime Cordial, and lime juice over ice until well chilled.
2. Strain into a chilled cocktail or coupe glass to serve straight up, or over fresh ice in a rocks glass to serve on the rocks.
3. Garnish with cucumber wheel and lime twist.

★ **YIELD: ONE DRINK** ★

HORSERADISH VODKA (NEW ENGLANDER)

This horseradish vodka also makes a very spicy and delicious Bloody Mary, or could be served straight from the freezer in shot glasses or stemmed cordial glasses to accompany smoked, cured, or pickled fishes, or caviar and blinis.

1 pound (455 g) fresh horseradish root
1 bottle (1.75 L) of vodka

1. Wash horseradish root to remove dirt and debris. Peel carefully with a sharp knife and remove any damaged or "woody" spots.
2. Shred the horseradish carefully in a food processor fitted with a shredding blade. BE CAREFUL: Horseradish root gives off very noxious cough- and tear-inducing fumes. Opening the lid of the food processor is like setting off a tear gas bomb. (I actually wear ski goggles when I'm preparing this at home!)
3. Measure 2 cups (140 g) of shredded horseradish root and place into your infusion container. Top with full bottle of vodka. Seal tightly and allow to infuse for 48 to 72 hours.
4. Strain carefully and funnel into clean bottles for storage. Keep refrigerated.

★ **YIELD: 1.75 LITERS** ★

{ Oyster shooter variation: To make a New Englander shooter, place a shucked oyster in a shot glass and top with 1 ounce (30 ml) of Horseradish Vodka. Add a splash of tomato juice. Bottoms up! }

Oyster shooters

Oyster shooters are a unique use of your homemade infused spirits, served in a shot glass with a shucked oyster at the bottom. Some of the shooters are served with a splash of juice to flavor them, and others are simply served as is, or "naked." The briny oyster lends a bit of salt to these small savory one-dose cocktails, and the flavored spirits make for a delicious oyster/liquor delivery system.

CUCUMBER, LEMON & DILL GIN (THE LONDONER)

The aromatics of gin are a natural match for the refreshing flavor combination of cucumber, lemon, and dill. This infusion tastes faintly of a well-crafted homemade pickle. As an oyster shooter, the brininess of the oyster adds to that "pickled" effect. Served on the rocks, it's simply savory, and added to tomato juice, it's a different twist on the standard spicy Bloody Mary.

1 English cucumber (2 cups [238 g]), to be
    seeded, peeled, and sliced as per the photos
    below
8 leafy sprigs of dill, bruised
Zest of 2 lemons, removed with a vegetable peeler
1 bottle (750 ml) gin

1. Peel, seed and slice the cucumber into half-moon shapes (a, b).
2. Bruise the dill, laying it between sheets of paper towels and rolling over it with a rolling pin (c).
3. Place the cucumber, lemon zest, and dill in an infusion jar (d).
4. Cover completely with gin (e).
5. Allow to infuse for 48 to 72 hours. Strain and funnel into clean bottle for storage. Keep refrigerated.

★ YIELD: APPROXIMATELY 750 ML ★

{ OYSTER SHOOTER VARIATION: To make a Londoner shooter, place a shucked oyster in a shot glass and top with 1¼ ounces (37 ml) of cucumber/lemon/dill infused gin. Serve as is. }

a   b   c   d   e

Bloody Mary Nichols

This is a very simple variation on a Bloody Mary, named in honor of Jack the Ripper's first identified victim. These can also be served as a brunch martini, shaken until well chilled, strained into a cocktail glass, and served "up."

2 ounces (60 ml) Cucumber, Lemon, and Dill Gin (opposite)
5 ounces (150 ml) plain tomato juice
Garnish: Cucumber spear, lemon wedge, and sprig of dill

1. Pour gin and tomato juice over ice in a collins glass.
2. Stir to mix ingredients thoroughly.
3. Garnish with cucumber spear, lemon wedge, and sprig of dill.

★ YIELD: ONE DRINK ★

★ INFUSIONS WITH A KICK ★

For cocktail enthusiasts that enjoy a bit of heat, the drinks on the following pages will please their spicy palettes. But more than just provide heat, the cocktails are complex and pair savory, spicy, and sweet together in innovative ways.

SERAFIN (SERRANO PEPPER AND TARRAGON—INFUSED TEQUILA)

This combination came about after a conversation about infusions with mixologist Gary Regan. He had told me about a pineapple, serrano pepper, and tarragon infusion that he had enjoyed at the Lark Creek Inn in Larkspur, California. There, Chef Bradley Ogden makes their infusion with reposado tequila and uses fresh pineapple chunks along with the fresh tarragon and serrano peppers to make a spicy and savory sipping tequila. The name *serafin* translates as "the fiery one."

4 serrano chili peppers, split and seeds removed, cut into rings (do with gloves)
10 sprigs of tarragon, bruised
1 bottle (1.75 L) silver tequila

1. Place the peppers and tarragon in a clean infusion jar.
2. Top with the tequila. Allow to infuse for 48 to 72 hours
3. Strain and funnel into clean bottle for storage. Keep refrigerated.

★ YIELD: 1.75 LITERS ★

{ OYSTER SHOOTER VARIATION: To make a Serafin oyster shooter, place a shucked oyster in a shot glass and top with 1 ounce (30 ml) of infused tequila. Top with a splash of pineapple juice. }

Serafina Cocktail

The Serafin tequila also makes a very interesting and savory cocktail when served martini style. Sweet and hot is always a great flavor contrast, and somewhat unexpected in this format.

2½ ounces (75 ml) Serafin (above)
1 ounce (30 ml) pineapple juice
Splash of fresh lime juice
Garnish: Lime wedge

1. Add infused tequila, pineapple juice, and lime juice to an ice-filled shaker.
2. Shake until well chilled and strain into a cocktail or coupe glass.
3. Garnish with a lime wedge.

★ YIELD: ONE DRINK ★

CHIHUAHUA (JALAPEÑO-CILANTRO VODKA)

There are a lot of one-note spicy infusions out there, but the combination of jalapeño and cilantro tastes more complex and flavorful than just simple heat. The addition of the splash of tomato tames the heat a bit and the end result is reminiscent of freshly made salsa.

8 jalapeño peppers (or 4 small Thai chili peppers), split and seeds removed (do with gloves)
12 sprigs cilantro, rinsed and bruised
1 bottle (1.75 L) vodka

1. Place the peppers and cilantro in infusion jar.
2. Top with the vodka. Allow to infuse for 48 to 72 hours.
3. Strain and funnel into clean bottle for storage. Keep refrigerated.

★ **YIELD: 1.75 LITERS** ★

{ OYSTER SHOOTER VARIATION: To make a Chihuahua oyster shooter, place a shucked oyster in a shot glass and top with 1 ounce (30 ml) of Jalapeño-Cilantro Vodka. Add a splash of tomato juice. }

Rabid Chihuahua

This cocktail utilizes the spicy and herbaceous vodka and adds the sweet element of pineapple to the mix. This also makes for a very nice brunch cocktail.

1½ ounces (45 ml) Chihuahua (above)
½ ounce 15 ml) Simple Syrup (page 34)
¾ ounce (22 ml) fresh lime juice
2 ounces (60 ml) pineapple juice
Optional garnish: Candied chile pepper, or lime wedge

1. Add ingredients to a shaker and fill with ice.
2. Shake until well chilled and serve up in a cocktail or coupe glass.
3. Garnish, if desired, with a candied chile pepper on a stick or a lime wedge.

★ **YIELD: ONE DRINK** ★

Limoncello has been produced in Sorrento and the Amalfi Coast of Italy for many years. The closely guarded family recipes were passed down from generation to generation. The secret to the laser beam lemon flavor of limoncello lies in the Sorrento lemons that are used to produce it. Sorrento lemons have a thick, wrinkled skin with a distinctive perfumed scent. A satisfactory limoncello can be produced from almost any lemons, but it won't have the distinctive flavor of a true Amalfi-coast limoncello.

The zests can be removed from the fruit with either a vegetable peeler or microplane grater. The tiny microplaned shreds mean more surface area is exposed to the alcohol, so the infusion is much faster. The limoncello infusion can be finished in 10 to14 days using the microplane, but 3 to 4 weeks with the larger strips of zest produced by the vegetable peeler. Once the limoncello is finished, you can store it in the freezer, where it becomes viscous. It's delicious served straight out of the freezer in small cordial glasses as an after dinner digestivo, poured over ice cream, drizzled over pound cake and fresh berries, or as a "corrective" additive to your iced tea or lemonade.

{ Many people suggest making limoncello and infusions from Everclear, or pure grain alcohol. I have tried this and found that the end result is simply too harsh, regardless of how much it is diluted or sweetened. Ethyl alcohol was made for sterilizing laboratory equipment, not for human consumption. The best compromise is to use 100-proof vodka for your limoncello. You get excellent extraction from the extra alcohol, but the end result won't burn your esophagus on the way down. When you finally dilute the infusion with Simple Syrup and more water if desired, the final proof level is around 65–70 and is much more palatable. }

HOMEMADE LIMONCELLO

1 dozen lemons, washed and wiped clean
1 lime, washed and wiped clean
1 bottle (750 ml) 100 proof vodka (Smirnoff works well)
2 cups (475 ml) sugar
2 cups (475 ml) water
1 bottle (750 ml) 80 proof vodka
Optional: additional filtered or bottled water
Additional Simple Syrup (page 34)

1. Remove the zest from the lemons and the lime, using a microplane. Place the small shreds of peels into a clean airtight container and cover with 100-proof vodka.
2. Place the jar in a safe place for at least 2 weeks, giving it an occasional shake and sniff to check on it. You'll be able to see the vodka turning bright yellow as it pulls the flavorful oils from the peels. When the peels no longer look colorful and the vodka doesn't seem to be gaining any more visible color or scent, it's done. Two to four weeks is the usual time frame.

3. On the day you will be finishing the limoncello, make a simple syrup with the sugar and water. Allow to cool to room temperature.
4. Filter the lemony infusion through a fine-mesh strainer or cheesecloth into a large bottle or jar. Make certain to press down to remove all the vodka and oils that you can from the peels.
5. Add the cooled syrup to the strained infusion and stir to incorporate completely. Add the 80-proof vodka and stir to incorporate completely.
6. Taste the limoncello. If it seems too strong, add filtered water to taste in 2-ounce (60 ml) increments until it is to your taste. If it doesn't seem sweet enough add more Simple Syrup, also in 2-ounce increments, until it is rectified to your liking. It's really a matter of taste. The end result should have a definitive kick of pure lemon flavor, be fairly sweet, and no stronger than you feel comfortable drinking without coughing or burning your throat.
7. Funnel the limoncello into clean bottles, and allow it to rest for at least a week. The limoncello mellows a bit, and the flavors meld together when given a bit of time to rest. Store in the freezer for best results, or bottle and distribute as gifts to grateful friends.

★ **YIELD: APPROXIMATELY 1.5 LITERS** ★

Homemade Limoncello variation:

Arancello is an easy variation on limoncello. The procedure is identical, substituting the zest of 8 oranges for the lemons and lime.

LIME IN YOUR LIMONCELLO

This limoncello recipe was first given to me by an Italian restaurateur in Augsberg, Germany. I had the pleasure of eating dinner at his restaurant while visiting family that was living there. I had tried limoncello before, and knew a little bit about it. I asked how he managed to get the luscious fragrance in his limoncello without access to Sorrento lemons. The secret is to include the zest of one lime in each batch, he told me. He was kind enough to write down the recipe for me on a cocktail napkin, which I carried back carefully folded in my luggage, eager to try his recipe for myself. I made a batch as soon as I got home and I've been making it the same way ever since. It's simple, the end result is delicious, and it makes a wonderful gift for friends at the holidays. The hardest part is waiting for it to be finished.

★ AQUAVIT ★

Aquavit is Scandinavia's answer to Eastern European vodka. It is distilled from grain in Denmark and Sweden, and potatoes in Norway but is then flavored with spices, herbs, and fruit oils. It has been produced there since the sixteenth century. Aquavit's distinctive flavor comes from the blend of spices and herbs. The main spice is almost always caraway and/or dill, with the addition of anise, cumin, coriander, peppery grains of paradise, or even amber. In Norway it is aged in oak casks, where the barrel-aging process softens the spirit in the way that aging cognac accomplishes the same end. It takes on a golden color from the barrels, but color alone is not necessarily an indication of age, since the spices can add color to the infusion. In some cases artificial color is added.

Aquavit is often drunk at festivals and for holidays, when it accompanies appetizers like pickled herring, smoked and cured fishes, and salted cod balls. In Norway, it's the customary accompaniment to Christmas dinner, as it supposedly helps aid digestion of the rich fatty foods like mutton and pork ribs that are part of the traditional Norwegian Christmas feast. Aquavit is always accompanied with toasts and often by drinking songs. It's a very festive spirit.

This recipe was created after researching various aquavit recipes and seeing which spices were being used, what the proportions of those spices were, and what other elements were being added, like citrus zest, clove, and star anise. The small amount of sweetener added rounds out the aquavit and takes some of the harsh edges away. If you'd prefer your aquavit sweeter and more viscous, add up to four ounces (120 ml) of the simple syrup to each finished liter.

HOMEMADE AQUAVIT

3 tablespoons (20 g) caraway seed
2 tablespoons (13 g) dill seed
2 tablespoons (12 g) cumin seed
1 tablespoons (5 g) coriander seed
1 tablespoons (6 g) fennel seed
2 star anise
3 whole cloves
4 strips each, orange and lemon peel (no pith), removed with a vegetable peeler
8½ cups (2 L) good quality vodka (I use Laird's for this)
3 ounces (90 ml) Demerara Simple Syrup (page 34)

1. Preheat oven to 400°F (200°C). Place seeds on a foil-lined cookie sheet or sizzle plate. Toast lightly in the oven for 6 to 8 minutes, stirring every few minutes until warm and fragrant. Remove and cool slightly.
2. Crush seeds lightly with a rolling pin or large bottle and place into large airtight infusion jar. Add star anise, cloves, citrus peels, and cover with the vodka. Seal tightly and shake.
3. Store at room temperature for at least 2 and up to 4 full weeks—shake bottle every couple of days to expose the spices again.

4. Strain carefully through a fine-mesh strainer, chinoise, or a gold coffee filter and rebottle.
5. Add 1½ ounces (45 ml) Demerara Simple Syrup to each bottle and shake well to incorporate. Store in the freezer for best effect. This infusion can be stored at room temperature if you'd like.

This can be served Scandinavian style (ice cold in small stemmed cordial glasses), in a Bloody Viking with your favorite Bloody Mary mix, or in another cocktail of your choosing.

★ YIELD: 2 LITERS ★

Bloody Viking

The Bloody Viking is a spin on a Bloody Mary, using the lovely flavorful homemade aquavit as the spirit. It's a really savory twist on everyone's favorite brunch drink.

2 ounces (60 ml) Aquavit (opposite)
4 ounces (120 ml) Basic Bloody Mary Mix (page 125), or your favorite mix
Garnish: Lime wedge and olive

1. Add 2 ounces Aquavit to a shaker and fill with 4 ounces (120 ml) of Bloody Mary mix.
2. Shake and strain over fresh ice in a tall glass.
3. Garnish with a lime wedge and an olive.

★ YIELD: ONE DRINK ★

Rosalind Russell

Hollywood star Rosalind Russell was supposedly a fan of aquavit and gave this recipe to Lucius Beebe, the author of the *Stork Club Bar Book*, published in 1946.

2 ounces (60 ml) Aquavit (opposite)
1 ounce (30 ml) dry vermouth (I like Dolin for this particular cocktail)
Garnish: Lemon peel

1. Add Aquavit and vermouth to a shaker glass filled with ice and stir vigorously until well chilled.
2. Strain into a cocktail or coupe glass. Garnish with lemon peel, squeezed over the surface of the drink, rubbed on the rim of the glass and discarded.

★ YIELD: ONE DRINK ★

★ TEQUILA POR MI AMANTE ★

Tequila Por Mi Amante, or "Tequila for my Beloved" is a delicious infusion of seasonal strawberries in reposado tequila. The first mentions of this concoction occur in 1939, in Charles H. Baker's *Gentleman's Companion*. It's a simple, straightforward recipe requiring only the ripest strawberries available and a good bottle of 100% agave tequila. The only thing required is some patience, as it takes several weeks of infusing to really pull the fresh flavor out of the berries, but it's worth the wait. Even folks that swear they hate tequila have been won over by this sweet and wondrous infusion. It can be sipped simply on the rocks, enjoyed with a squeeze of lime and club soda, or incorporated into your favorite tequila cocktail, bringing a new dimension of summery berry flavor to any tried and true tequila cocktail.

Try substituting it into the Rosemary Paloma (page 45) for a truly unusual and delicious variation.

3 pints (870 g) ripe fragrant strawberries; washed, hulled,
**   and sliced into quarters or smaller if they're really large**
1 bottle (750 ml) of 100% agave reposado tequila

1. Place the washed, sliced berries into a clean airtight jar. Pour in tequila to cover. Agitate the jar gently so as not to break up the berries. Agitate the berries gently every other day.
2. Over the course of 2 to 4 weeks, the berries will have given up all of their color and flavor. Pour the tequila through a fine-mesh strainer lined with cheesecloth or a chinoise. Squeeze or press down until all the liquid is extracted. Discard the berries, because they've already provided all of their color and flavor.
3. If desired, you may strain it through the cheesecloth a few more times, removing all of the small pieces of seeds and berry, until the infusion is transparent. It should be a brilliant ruby red and very fragrant of strawberries.
4. Funnel the strained, infused tequila into clean bottles and refrigerate. Allow it to rest for at least a week to mellow.

Enjoy it either on the rocks, shaken and strained into a cocktail glass with a wedge of lime, or as an ingredient in your favorite tequila cocktail. It keeps for several weeks. Over time the flavor degrades as oxidation sets in, and the flavors aren't as fresh and perfumed as they were. I've never had this be a problem, however, as the Tequila Por Mi Amante is so appealing the problem is more often not having enough of it around.

★ **YIELD: 750 ML** ★

Strawberry Margarita

Rather than a storebought strawberry flavoring, the delicious natural strawberry flavor of Tequila Por Mi Amante makes the best flavored Margarita you'll ever have.

1¾ ounces (52 ml) Tequila Por Mi Amante (opposite)
1 ounce (30 ml) Cointreau or Triple Sec
¾ ounce (22 ml) fresh lime juice
Garnish: Lime wedge

1. Add ingredients to a cocktail shaker and fill with ice. Shake until well chilled.
2. Strain into a chilled cocktail glass to serve up or over fresh ice in a rocks glass to serve on the rocks.
3. Garnish with a lime wedge.

★ **YIELD: ONE DRINK** ★

★ BITTERS ★

The truest sign of a devout cocktail nerd isn't how well stocked their bar is with spirits, but how well stocked it is with bitters.

Bitters are to cocktails as salt is to soup. A few drops are all it takes to bring the balance together and make it seem like the flavors are greater than the sum of their parts. Adding a few drops of bitters to your cocktail is like tuning the picture on an old black-and-white television with rabbit-ear antennae. It brings everything together into focus so it's better, clearer, and easier to understand.

While it used to be that there were only one or two kinds of bitters available, there is now an embarrassment of riches available, with wide-ranging flavors from fruity to savory. Just as I began to collect exotic salts and spices as my cooking skills improved, my collection of bitters has grown exponentially as I've bartended longer and begun to understand the construction of cocktail flavors better.

»» The History of Bitters ««

Cocktail bitters have been around since the early nineteenth century, and many of them actually started out as patent medicines and digestifs even earlier than that. Adding bitters to a cocktail is part of the definition of a cocktail; bitters differentiates it from a "sling," or simply spirit(s) and water with flavoring and/or sweetening added.

Most bitters are composed of a tincture of high-proof alcohol infused with bitter and/or aromatic herbs, spices, roots, or barks such as chinchona, gentian, quassia, cardamom, aniseed, citrus peels, or wormwood. Many of these bitter botanicals had been used for centuries medicinally as antinausea or antifever medications, so adding them to spirits to soothe whatever malady was ailing you was a logical next step. In the late nineteenth century there were dozens of bitters brands available, and many bars made their own house bitters as well.

The granddaddy of all cocktail bitters and certainly the most omnipresent are Angostura bitters, invented by Dr. Johann Gottlieb Benjamin Siegert, a German physician and scientist who was Surgeon General of the military hospital in Angostura, Venezuela, under Simon Bolivar. (Note: There is also a bark called Angostura, which is named for the same town, that is used as a bittering agent in several brands of cocktail bitters, but ironically, not in Angostura *brand* bitters.)

In seeking a remedy for the fevers and stomach ailments of the battle-battered soldiers, Dr. Siegert used his scientific training to research and analyze the plethora of tropical herbs and plants that were available to him. In 1824, he finally settled on a unique formula he named *Amargo Aromatico*, or aromatic bitters. His bitters proved popular both with his patients and immediate friends and family as well as the constant stream of habitually seasick sailors who passed through this Orinoco River port city. Soon these sailors were taking Dr. Siegert's Angostura bitters back to their home countries, and the beginnings of a commercial enterprise were taking shape. In 1830, a distillery was built to keep up with the increasing demand for the product.

Eventually Dr. Siegert's sons Carlos and Alfredo moved the company to nearby Trinidad in 1875, where it remains to this day. The company later added distilling rum to their portfolio. The trademark yellow-capped bottles with the oversized text-laden labels can be seen in virtually every bar in the civilized world.

Angostura is used in several classic cocktails. It's the starter ingredient in Pink Gin, so named for the color it turns the drink. A proper Manhattan or Champagne Cocktail can't be made without Angostura. It's a key ingredient in many tiki- and rum-based cocktails such as the Trinidad Sour and is sprinkled on top of a Pisco Sour both for aromatics and decoration.

Another bitters with medicinal roots is Peychaud's bitters, created in 1830 by Antoine Amédée Peychaud, a Haitian apothecary who had settled in New Orleans. Mssr. Peychaud's after-hours experiments eventually led to his mixing his bitters with brandy and pastis. This later evolved famously into the Sazerac cocktail, the drink for which these bitters are most well known. Unlike the dessert spice–heavy Angostura bitters, the sweeter and more floral anise and vanilla flavors of Peychaud's work well in brandy- and rye-based drinks, and are *de rigueur* in the Vieux Carre and the Cocktail à la Louisiane, two other enduring New Orleans classic cocktails. Peychaud's bitters also bring a festive bright red color to any drink they are added to.

»» Orange Bitters ««

Orange bitters popped up during the bitters (r)evolution of the nineteenth century. Although bitter orange–based liqueurs such as Cointreau and other orange Curaçaos were often added to cocktails as a sweetening agent, orange bitters were like a more concentrated version of this, and added a new spicy and floral character with a familiar flavor profile to many different drinks such as Brandy Crustas and the Martinez. Orange bitters were considered a staple ingredient in gin martinis in the early days.

{ One of my favorite bartender "tricks" is to add just a drop or two of orange bitters to a gin martini to intensify the flavors and add that *je ne sais quoi* that always makes customers ask why this martini is so much better than the ones they're usually served. In addition to being an excellent complement to the herbaceous flavors in gin, orange bitters have a real affinity for herbal flavors such as those found in Chartreuse, Benedictine, and vermouths. }

Orange bitters were close to going the way of the dodo not so long ago. Fee Brothers, a Rochester, New York–based company that is now under the stewardship of the fourth generation of the Fee family, had kept the style viable with their West Indian Orange Bitters. Renowned bartender/cocktail and spirits writer Gary Regan added his own version to the alternatives in 1995, when he developed Regans' Orange Bitters #6, which are produced by the Sazerac company. Regan's No. 6 bitters has a drier flavor and stronger spicy edge than the Fee Brothers.

Many bartenders will mix the Fee Brothers and Regan's orange bitters 50/50 in a dropper or dasher bottle to get the best characteristics of both. If you do this, keep the bottles of the original formulas around to compare and contrast in the same cocktail, which can be quite an enlightening experience. Angostura also recently introduced an orange bitters that is quite delicious, and lighter in flavor than the other existing orange bitters brands, which could merit purchasing on their own if you find other orange bitters too strong for your liking.

{ Phoebe recommends an excellent means of "tasting" bitters. She suggests dropping a couple of dashes into your palm, rubbing your palms together, and holding them up to your face so you can inhale the aromatics. Since alcoholic bitters are generally bottled at a fairly high proof level, this is a way to experience the flavors without the burn of the alcohol. }

»» Classic Style, New Flavors ««

The resurgence of cocktail craftsmanship has led to a veritable explosion in the bitters available for both the professional and the home bartending enthusiast. There are many new flavors of bitters being created by both established producers such as Fee Brothers, as well as newer companies like Bittermens, The Bitter Truth, Scrappy's Bitters, Bitters, Old Men, Urban Moonshine, A.B. Smeby Bittering Company, and Bittercube.

★ Other citrus flavors such as grapefruit, lemon, and lime are available, as well as celery bitters, chocolate, rhubarb, plum, cardamom, root beer, and lavender bitters, just to name a few.

★ Flavors that were formulated for specific uses such as the Bittermens Elemakule Tiki cocktail bitters or their chamomile and citrus-based Boston Bittahs, which were formulated to pair with gin, are becoming more and more common.

★ One of the most fascinating new bitters manufacturing tales comes from Adam Elmegirab, an Aberdeen, Scotland-based bartender. He took it upon himself to research and recreate the formula of original Boker's bitters, a long-forgotten bitters formula that had been extinct since Prohibition, but was prominently mentioned in Professor Jerry Thomas's 1862 bartender's guide, *How to Mix Drinks or The Bon Vivant's Companion*.

»» Making Your Own Bitters ««

Making bitters is just like making any other infusion. In fact, the only challenge may be tracking down some of the more esoteric botanicals in some recipes. (The bitters recipe on page 149 calls for readily available ingredients.) There are plenty of online sources for these ingredients, and they are also available at some herbalist shops and apothecary shops in larger urban areas.

The basic procedure for making bitters involves steeping a bittering agent either separately or with the aromatics, and agitating them at least once daily for several days to several weeks. Strain the solids from the tincture, dilute the mixture, and then bottle it. *Voilà!* Homemade bitters.

Making your own bitters may take a few tries to get things exactly as you wish them to be… but that can be fun, too. Remember that patience is a virtue, most particularly when making infusions of any sort. Make small batches, measure accurately, and take meticulous notes as you go along. Once you have a recipe fine tuned you can either multiply your proportions to make a bigger batch, or combine multiple batches. Think of it as a science lab. The absolute worst that can happen is you'll create something that tastes, well, *bitter*. At best, your new bitters might become the next Angostura.

SPICE BITTERS (Courtesy of Phoebe Esmon, The Farmer's Cabinet, Philadelphia, PA)

1 ounce (30 ml) black tea (any style; used as a bittering agent)
1 bottle (750 ml) Old Grand-Dad bonded bourbon, or other overproof bourbon
2 cinnamon sticks, crushed
10 cloves
2 allspice berries
1 nutmeg berry
1 star anise pod, bruised
1 piece (1 inch, or 2.5 cm) vanilla bean

In addition to the ingredients listed above, have on hand: Two clean airtight jars with lids (quart mason jars are good for this purpose), fine-mesh strainer or reusable cone coffee filter, unbleached paper coffee filters, two clean bowls or containers to strain into, distilled water, clean dasher or dropper bottles, and a small funnel.

1. To prepare the bittering agent, first place the black tea of your choosing in its own jar.
2. Add about 5 ounces (150 ml) bourbon, seal tightly, and place in a warm spot, such as a window, to infuse.
3. To prepare the aromatics, place all other ingredients in another jar, pour in the rest of the bourbon, and place in a warm place to infuse.
4. Shake each jar twice daily for 10 days. After 10 days, strain out the ingredients. The best way to strain your ingredients, leaving the least particulate matter behind, is to use a plastic cone-style coffee maker and an unbleached paper coffee filter. Use separate paper filters and containers to strain both the bittering agent and the spice infusion into separate clean containers.
5. Add the bittered bourbon to the spiced infusion until you are satisfied with the bitterness level. Set aside any leftovers, which can be used in your next batch.
6. To cut and bottle, measure the volume of your final product and add an equal volume of distilled water. By diluting your bitters in half with water, you make the flavor of the final product less bitter as well as bring the final proof level down to something palatable that won't throw off the balance of a cocktail. Funnel into clean bottles, either dasher bottles or dropper bottles, whichever you prefer to use. Bitters bottles can be purchased online, or repurposed from other bitters by soaking off the labels and cleaning and sterilizing in boiling water. These will keep indefinitely, due to the still significant percentage of alcohol in the end product.

Phoebe recommends using these bitters in any cocktail that contains fresh-muddled stone fruit, berries, or fruit or berry syrups. A few drops of these bitters would be delicious in the Smoked Peach Bourbon Smash (page 42) or the Blueberry Lemonade (page 82), for example.

★ YIELD: APPROXIMATELY 750 ML ★

FLAVOR VARIATIONS

A bit of advanced research into which bittering agent is most appealing to you is the best starting point:

★ chinchona or quinine (like tonic water)
★ gentian (Angostura)
★ wormwood (earthy absinthe)
★ garam masala
★ dried orange, lemon, and grapefruit peels

Remember, making bitters is like a science lab—experiment! After you've decided which flavorings to use, you can choose a high-proof solvent in which you will make your tincture. Everclear, or pure ethyl alcohol, is not legal for purchase everywhere, but will give you the blankest slate upon which to layer your flavors. If you want more complexity and a sweeter background note in your bitters, a high-proof rum (such as Lemon Hart or Wray & Nephew) is a good base. If you like the sophisticated, smooth flavors of barrel-aged spirits, then try overproof bourbon as your base.

Now that you have an idea of what you'll need to start making homegrown cocktails, here is a guide to some of my favorite sources of equipment, ingredients, and inspiration.

BAR AND KITCHEN TOOLS

The best place to start looking is your local bar and restaurant supply store, where commercial-grade shakers, jiggers, spoons, glassware, and anything else you might need are available at wholesale prices. Online searches will yield multiple results. The housewares section of your local department store or larger kitchen/housewares retailers have essentially anything you need.

★ BOSTON SHAKER
http://store.thebostonshaker.com
Bar tools, cocktailware, bitters, garnishes, and other ingredients. A wide variety of bottles for storage and dispensing. Not inexpensive, but an excellent selection.

★ FANTE'S
http://fantes.com
A fixture in Philadelphia's Italian Market since 1906, Fante's has an extensive collection of kitchen equipment, barware, and tools for both kitchen and bar. Prices are competitive and the selection is wide ranging.

★ HOME WET BAR
www.homewetbar.com
Bar tools, glassware, accessories, and an excellent selection of home bar décor items.

★ KEG WORKS
www.kegworks.com
One of the most comprehensive selections of everything from commercial-grade blenders and juice extractors, to bar tools, glassware, cocktail bitters, and bar accessories to make your home bar feel like your favorite neighborhood pub.

★ OXO TOOLS
www.oxo.com
Measuring cups, angled easy-read jiggers, vegetable peelers, shakers, and muddlers.

UPSCALE AND SPECIALTY TOOLS

★ COCKTAIL KINGDOM
http://www.cocktailkingdom.com
The ultra source for any and all things bar related. Shakers, mixing glasses, spoons, dasher bottles, bitters, and more to outfit your bar. Excellent selection of cocktail books.

★ PUG MUDDLERS
http://wnjones.com/pug
Hand-turned wooden muddlers that are the custom Louisville Sluggers of the bar set. Not only beautiful to look at, but very effective tools for the job.

★ ÜBER BAR TOOLS
http://uberbartools.com
Extremely well-made and stylish bar strainers, bar spoons, muddlers, and smart jiggers called Bar Bones or Pro Jigs that have various measurements on slick one-piece units. Excellent videos in the Tutorials section.

HERBS, SPICES, AND BOTANICALS

Growing your own herbs and produce in your garden is the best source for fresh and local. If you are "plant impaired" or have a black thumb (as I seem to), seek out a local herb and spice purveyor that has fresh products and high turnover. There are several reliable online sources for herbs and spices:

★ DANDELION BOTANICAL COMPANY
www.dandelionbotanical.com
Dandelion Botanical Company is a family-owned herbal apothecary specializing in high-quality botanicals. It is an excellent resource for difficult-to-source ingredients for homemade bitters.

★ MOUNTAIN ROSE HERBS
www.mountainroseherbs.com
This Eugene, Oregon-based company sells only certified organic herbs, spices, and botanicals. The products are always fresh and fragrant, and the company is committed to sustainable farming practices, fair trade, and green packaging and promotional materials. An excellent source for harder-to-find botanicals such as ingredients for bitters.

★ PACIFIC BOTANICALS
www.pacificbotanicals.com
High quality certified organic herbs and spices, plus fresh herbs in season.

★ PENZEYS SPICES
www.penzeys.com
Extensive catalog of herbs, spices, seasoning blends, extracts, and botanicals. Convenient packaging from small jars to large bulk bags. Check the website for store locations near you.

FLAVORS, EXTRACTS, AND BITTERS
Your local specialty food store, grocer, or ethnic market should have most of these items available. Here are some excellent online sources:

★ DIBRUNO BROTHERS
www.dibruno.com
Another Philadelphia Italian Market institution, DiBruno Brothers has been around since 1939 and carries a wide selection of bitters, extracts, flavorings, and vinegars for use in cocktails and culinary applications.

★ KALUSTYAN'S
http://kalustyans.com
A landmark specialty foods importer and grocer in New York City, Kalustyan's carries herbs, spices, sugars, ethnic flavorings, and extracts.

COCKTAIL BITTERS
Some bitters mentioned in this book are only available directly from the source.

★ A.B. SMEBY BITTERING CO.
http://absmebybitteringco.com
All natural, seasonal bitters, handcrafted in Brooklyn, New York. Interesting flavor combinations include Apple Cinnamon with Molasses, Licorice-Nectarine, and Highland Heather.

★ THE BITTER TRUTH
http://the-bitter-truth.com
This German bitters company is the brainchild of Munich bartenders Stephan Berg and Alexander Hauck. A wide range of bitters, spirits, and liqueurs available ranging from single flavor citrus bitters like orange, lemon, and grapefruit, their award-winning celery bitters to aromatic bitters and recreations of vintage bitters formulas such as their Jerry Thomas Decanter bitters. Nice selection of cocktail recipes featuring their bitters is on the website.

★ BITTERCUBE
http://bittercube.com
Handcrafted bitters from bartenders Nicholas Kosevich and Ira Koplowitz, the company is based in Milwaukee, Wisconsin. Bitters are made using only raw ingredients, and no extracts. Blackstrap Molasses and Cherry Bark bitters seem quite intriguing and original.

★ BITTERMENS
http://bittermens.com
Small batch bitters and shrubs, primarily exotic combination flavors such as Xocolatl Mole bitters and 'Elemakule Tiki Cocktail bitters.

★ BITTERS, OLD MEN
http://bittersoldmen.com
Handmade in Manhattan, with an interesting lineup of flavors such as papaya, peach-basil, and Isaan Another Level, which includes spicy elements of Isaan Thai cuisine.

★ FEE BROTHERS
www.feebrothers.com
Extensive selection of bitters, cordial syrups, and cocktail flavorings shipped direct from Rochester, New York, since 1863.

★ SCRAPPY'S BITTERS
http://scrappysbitters.com
All natural, handmade bitters by Seattle-based bartender Miles Thomas, in a variety of single citrus and herbal flavors, including lavender and cardamom.

★ URBAN MOONSHINE
http://www.urbanmoonshine.com
Handmade organic bitters, tonics, and tinctures formulated by herbalist Jovial King in Burlington, Vermont. Bitters flavors include original bitters, citrus, and maple.

BOTTLES, DROPPERS, AND CONTAINERS
While empty screw-capped wine bottles that are well washed and have the labels removed work just fine for storing your homemade creations, sometimes you want a more professional-looking presentation, either for your home bar or for gifting. Dasher bottles and eyedroppers come in handy for your own bitters or to use for dispensing small quantities at your bar. Small atomizer bottles are useful for spraying aromatics on the surface of your cocktails, and lightly and evenly coating a glass with vermouth or absinthe rather than "rinsing" the glass or the "in and out" method which inevitably leaves a puddle at the bottom of the glass and will make the last sip taste very different from the first.

★ EBOTTLES
www.ebottles.com

Wholesale pricing and a wide selection of well-made bottles for basically any purpose. Excellent selection of closures, including shrink-wrap tops you can put on with a blow dryer to professionally seal your creations.

★ SPECIALTY BOTTLE
www.specialtybottle.com

Bottle suppliers to many large catalog companies, Specialty Bottle has no minimum orders, competitive prices, and excellent customer service. There's a wide selection of bottles in all styles and colors, as well as jars for storing spices, sauces, and other needs for the creative cook.

INFORMATION AND INSPIRATION: COCKTAIL DATABASES AND BLOGS

There are so many cocktail recipe websites and cocktail blogs that I couldn't even begin to scratch the surface of that long list, but here are a few of my favorite places to find information and inspiration when I need it.

★ BEACHBUM BERRY
http://beachbumberry.com

Jeff "Beachbum" Berry is one of the world's foremost historians and authorities on all things related to tiki and exotic cocktails. His website explores drink recipes, tiki culture, and travel.

★ THE CHANTICLEER SOCIETY
http://chanticleersociety.org

The sister site to Drinkboy.com, the Chanticleer Society website is a worldwide discussion group for mixologists, spirits journalists, and cocktail enthusiasts.

★ THE COCKTAIL CHRONICLES
www.cocktailchronicles.com

Excellent web log by cocktail and spirits journalist Paul Clarke. Paul is also a contributing editor at *Imbibe* magazine. Recipes, articles, and discussion of cocktails, spirits, and drinking culture in general, as well as host/moderator for Mixology Monday, a virtual cocktail party where everyone gets to contribute a recipe for discussion based on that week's theme.

★ COCKTAILDB
www.cocktaildb.com

Martin Doudoroff and Ted (Dr. Cocktail) Haigh created the cocktaildb database and it is the largest repository of verified cocktail recipes online. Excellent search features include the ability to search by drink name or search by included ingredients. The Mixilator feature will randomly generate a cocktail for you based on the criteria you specify.

★ DRINKBOY.COM
www.drinkboy.com

Drinkboy.com is the brainchild of cocktail and spirits enthusiast Robert Hess. It includes links to articles, book reviews, listings of spirits and ingredients, and of course, cocktail recipes.

★ KINDRED COCKTAILS
www.kindredcocktails.com

Cocktail recipe database that is the shared creation of the membership, which includes both professionals and cocktail enthusiasts. Kindred cocktails allows you to share your original recipes, search for recipes, and create your own personal recipe database within the site, thereby saving your favorites so you need not search for them every time you want to make one.

★ SMALL SCREEN NETWORK
www.smallscreennetwork.com

Hands down the best source for informative cocktail how-to videos and educational content. Several different shows to choose from, each with engaging and instructive hosts.

★ TALES OF THE COCKTAIL
www.talesofthecocktail.com

The foremost cocktail festival in the world, held every July in New Orleans. While many professionals are in attendance, there are many home cocktail enthusiasts as well. Seminars, dinners, and tastings appeal to anyone with a serious academic interest in cocktails and cocktail culture.

ABOUT THE AUTHOR

Katie M. Loeb was born in New York City and grew up in Teaneck, New Jersey. She moved to Philadelphia to attend the University of Pennsylvania as an undergraduate, fell in love with the city, and decided to make it her permanent home. Even before graduating with a degree in communications and marketing, she began working in the telecommunications industry for several years but found her passion when she began working for a catering company on the weekends. After changing careers to concentrate full time in the restaurant and beverage industry, she has worn many hats—server, manager, bartender, beverage director, and controller. She is a sommelier, creator of craft cocktails, and author of numerous articles and cocktail recipes, which have been published in *Bon Appétit,* the *Los Angeles Times, Imbibe, Philadelphia Magazine, Inside,* and *Food & Wine Magazine* cocktail books. She has consulted for numerous restaurant groups and spirit brands, providing cocktail recipes, beverage lists, and operations assistance. This is her first cocktail book featuring the house-made ingredients for which she has become known.

About the Photographer

Steve Legato's passion for photography has granted him the humbling opportunity to work with some of the most dedicated, passionate, and creative chefs you've heard of and dozens you haven't heard of—yet. His photography has been featured in *Art Culinaire,* the *New York Times, Bon Appétit, GQ, Wine Spectator, Food Arts, Travel & Leisure,* and *Wine & Spirits.* He has photographed more than thirty cookbooks, including *!Ceviche!* by Guillermo Pernot, which won a James Beard Award in 2002, and *Nicholas: The Restaurant,* which was nominated for the 2010 IACP Cookbook award for photography. **www.stevelegato.com**

★★★★★★★★ ACKNOWLEDGMENTS ★★★★★★★★★★★★★★

A very special thanks to my mom, Iris, for raising me right and teaching me to make her a perfect Manhattan when I was about 6 years old. She always told me I could do anything I set my mind to. Look where that combination of lessons has gotten me. This book is dedicated to her.

To my family of friends, thank you for being in my corner in every way and always supporting me in all that I do. Your encouragement, willingness to play taste testers for me, and most of all your unconditional love truly means the world to me.

My thanks to Clare Pelino and the team at ProLiterary for putting me in touch with the folks at Quarry Books, and helping me through the process.

To the editing team at Quarry—Rochelle Bourgault, Jennifer Grady and Tiffany Hill—thanks for making me look so smart! Thanks to David Martinell and the Art Department at Quarry for putting it all together so stunningly.

A huge thank you to Steve Legato, for stellar photography and friendship throughout this process. I know what I see when the photo is set up, but what he sees through his lens is always so much more beautiful.

Thank you to the Brendle family—Glenn, Karen, and Ian, and Barbie Marshall—for allowing Steve and I to come out to Green Meadow Farm and taking so much time out of their busy schedule to help us with the photo shoot with photo styling, borrowing of glassware and scenery, camaraderie and disposal of finished cocktails. This book wouldn't be the same without your generosity.

Thank you Jose Garces, for believing in me first as your employee and later as your friend. I've learned so much from you and continue to do so.

My thanks to all of the kind folks that either donated or discounted products to me for recipe development and/or photo shoots, or loaned me items for the same. My sincere thanks go to Michael Anastasio Produce, Fante's, DiBruno Brothers, Mountain Rose Herbs, and Fee Brothers. It all came in handy, believe me.

To my friends in the bartending community that contributed recipes and advice for this book, I could not have done this without you. Jeff Berry, Jamie Boudreau, Barbara Marshall and Ian Brendle, Phoebe Esmon, Andrea Fleegle, Maggie Meskey, Maria Polise, Ryan Reigel, Audrey Saunders, thanks for your recipes and assistance. To all of my bartending cohorts and past and present employers, thanks for making me think harder and work harder. I wouldn't be the bartender I am today without your encouragement and striving to meet the exacting standards that you have all set for me to aspire to.

A

absinthe
  bitters and, 150
  Rhum Ricardo, 117
  wormwood and, 15
agave nectar, 27
Agave Tequila, 12
Allspice Dram. See Pimento (or Allspice) Dram.
Amargo Aromatico, 146
Amaro Averna liqueur, 81
añejo rums, 11
añejo tequila, 12
Angostura bitters
  Falernum, 117
  Lion's Tail, 119
  Melon-choly Baby, 67
  Money Manhattan, 127
  Naughty Pilgrim, 59
  Pimento (or Allspice) Dram, 118
  Pink Sapphire Swizzle, 113
aperitifs, 15–16
apple dividers, 25
applejack
  Jack Rose, 96
  Naughty Pilgrim, 59
Aquavit, 142–143
Arancello, 141

B

Baker, Charles H., 144
Bark and Blood, 62
bar spoons, 17, 19
bar tools, 17–19
Basic Bloody Mary Mix, 121, 143
Basic Herbal Cooler, 55
Basic Hot Toddy, 60
Benedictine
  introduction, 16
  orange bitters and, 147
  Piña Doble, 84–85
Berry, Jeff "Beachbum," 89
Better Bellini, 81
"Birdbath" glasses, 20
bitters
  Angostura, 59, 67, 113, 117, 118, 119, 127
  barrel-aged, 127
  creating, 148
  flavor variations, 150
  grapefruit, 71, 79
  history of, 146
  introduction, 145
  lemon bitters, 46, 48, 79
  modern flavors, 148
  orange bitters, 42, 61, 113, 147
  spice bitters, 149
  "tasting," 147
Blackberry Shrub, 90

Black Currant–Kaffir Lime "Grenadine," 98, 100
blanco tequila, 12, 45
blended whiskeys, 14
blenders, 19, 24
Blood Mary Nichols, 137
Bloody Viking, 143
Blueberry Lemonade, 82, 149
Blueberry Syrup, 82
Boudreau, Jamie, 45
bourbon
  Basic Herbal Cooler, 55
  Basic Hot Toddy, 60
  introduction, 13
  Lion's Tail, 119
  Mint Julep, 43
  Money Manhattan, 127
  Orange-Cardamom Cooler, 68–69
  Port Light, 89
  Smoked Peach Bourbon Smash, 42
  Spice Bitters, 149
brandy
  Basic Hot Toddy, 60
  Cocktail Cherries, 124
  Man-Full-O'-Trouble Punch, 53
  Naughty Pilgrim, 59
  Orgeat Syrup, 114
  snifters, 20
Brendle, Ian, 50
brown sugars, 27

C

Canción de Flores, 50
canning jars, 21
carbonation machines, 23
Cardamom-Kaffir Lime Syrup, 63–64
Celery Syrup, 73–74
champagne
  Better Bellini, 81
  Canción de Flores, 50
  coupe glasses, 20
  Love in Bloom, 52
  vinegar, 122
Champagne Flute glasses, 20
channel knives, 17, 18
Chartreuse, 16
cherries, 22–23, 25, 124–125, 127
cherry liqueur, 124
cherry pitters, 25
Chihuahua Infusion, 139
Cinnamon Syrup, 60–62
citric acid powder, 31

citrus cordials
  Fresh Lime Cordial, 106–108
  introduction, 101
  Lemon Cordial, 103–105
  Ruby Red Grapefruit-Lemongrass Cordial, 102
citrus juices, 22
citrus presses, 17
citrus twists, 17, 18
citrus zesters, 17, 18
cocktail glasses, 20
Cocktail Guide and Ladies' Companion (Crosby Gaige), 119
cocktail onions, 23, 122–123
cocktail starters. See also syrups.
  Basic Bloody Mary Mix, 121
  Pimento (or Allspice) Dram, 118–119
coffee grinders, 25
cognac
  Benedictine, 16, 84–85, 147
  Cocktail Cherries, 124
  introduction, 15
  Man-Full-O'-Trouble Punch, 53
  None But the Brave, 119
  Orgeat Syrup, 114
colanders, 24
colas, 22
Cold-Process Grenadine, 94
commercial-grade blenders, 24
community-supported agriculture, 29
corn whiskey, 13
Coupe glasses, 20
Cucumber Gimlet, 134
Cucumber, Lemon & Dill Gin Infusion, 136–137
Cucumber Vodka/Gin Infusion, 133–134
Curaçao
  Mai Tai, 116
  orange Curaçao, 15, 116, 147
cutting boards, 17

D

Dark 'n' Stormy, 112
Dark Rums, 11
Demerara Simple Syrup, 34, 117, 119, 142
demerara sugar, 27
Dessert Spiced Syrup, 56, 59–60

E

electric juicers, 23
Elmegirab, Adam, 148
Esmon, Phoebe, 149
Everclear, 150
Extra Añejo Tequila, 12

F

Falernum, 113, 117
The Farmer's Cabinet restaurant
 and bar, 149
farmers' markets, 29, 30
Fee Brothers, 147
flaming technique, 62
Fleegle, Andrea, 44
Fresh Lemon Gimlet, 103, 105
Fresh Lime Cordial, 106–108, 134
Fresh Lime Gimlet, 108
Front Stoop Lemonade, 39, 103
fruit juices, 22
fruit/vegetable syrups
 Blackberry Shrub, 90
 Blueberry Syrup, 82
 Celery Syrup, 73–74
 Passion Fruit Syrup, 86–89
 Peach Syrup, 80–81
 Pear Syrup, 76–79
 Rhubarb Syrup, 70–71

G

Gaige, Crosby, 119
garnishes. See cocktail garnishes.
Gentleman's Companion
 (Charles H. Baker), 144
Gibson, 123
Gimlette, Sir Thomas D., 101
gin
 Basic Herbal Cooler, 55
 Bloody Mary Nichols, 137
 Cucumber Gimlet, 134
 Cucumber Gin Infusion, 133–134
 Cucumber, Lemon & Dill Gin
  Infusion, 136–137
 Dark 'n' Stormy, 112
 Fresh Lemon Gimlet, 105
 Fresh Lime Gimlet, 108
 Front Stoop Lemonade, 39
 Gibson, 123
 Gin-Gin Mule, 112
 The GMF, 50
 The Grape Gatsby, 64
 introduction, 10–11
 London dry gin, 10
 Melon-choly Baby, 67
 "new generation" gins, 10–11
 Orange-Cardamom Cooler,
  68–69
 Parisian Martini, 46
 Pink Sapphire Swizzle, 113
 Plymouth gin, 10
 Provençal Martini, 48
 Purple Haze, 100
 Royster Cup, 74
 Salty Pomeranian, 107

ginger beer
 Homemade Ginger Beer
  Concentrate, 59, 109, 111–113
 introduction, 109
Ginger Syrup, 66–67
Gin-Gin Mule, 112
glassware, 20–21
The GMF, 50
Gosling's Brothers Limited, 112
Grand Marnier liqueur, 53
The Grape Gatsby, 64
Green Chartreuse, 16
Green Meadow Farm, 50
Grenadine
 Black Currant–Kaffir Lime, 98,
  100
 cold process, 94
 Homemade Grenadine, 86, 89,
  94, 95, 96, 97
 hot process, 95
grill-top smokers, 25
grinders, 25
Grog Log (Jeff "Beachbum"
 Berry), 89

H

Hemingway Daiquiri, 102
herbal syrups
 herbs, purchasing, 30
 Hibiscus Syrup, 51–53
 Honeysuckle Syrup, 49–50
 introduction, 37
 Lavender Syrup, 47–48
 Mint Syrup, 40–43
 Mixed Herb Syrup, 54–55
 Rosemary Syrup, 44–45
 Thai Basil Syrup, 38–39, 113
 Thyme Syrup, 46
Hibiscus Syrup, 51–53
Highball glasses, 20
Homemade Aquavit, 142–143
Homemade Ginger Beer Concen-
 trate, 59, 109, 111–113
Homemade Grenadine, 86, 89, 94,
 95, 96, 97, 98
Homemade Limoncello, 140–141
Honeysuckle Syrup, 49–50
Horseradish Vodka, 135
Hot Apple Pie, 61
Hot-Process Grenadine, 95
Hurricane, 86

I

infusions
 Aquavit, 142–143
 base spirits, 129, 130
 Chihuahua, 139
 creating, 130

Cucumber, Lemon & Dill Gin,
 136–137
Cucumber Vodka/Gin Infusions,
 133–134
Horseradish Vodka, 135
ingredient selection, 130
introduction, 129
jar selection, 130
Limoncello, 140–141
Pineapple Vodka, 132–133
Serafin, 138
storage, 131, 140
straining, 131
Tequila Por Mi Amante, 144–145

J

Jack Rose, 96
Jalapeño-Cilantro Vodka. *See*
 Chihuahua Infusion.
Jalisco Cel-Ray, 74
jelly jars, 21
jiggers, 17, 19
Joven Tequila, 12
juicers, 17, 23
juices, 22

K

Kahiki Supper Club, 89
kitchen tools, 23, 24–26
knives, 17, 18, 25

L

ladles, 25
Lark Creek Inn, 138
Lavender Lemonade, 47
Lavender Syrup, 47–48
Lemon Cordial, 39, 103–105
Limoncello, 140–141
Lion's Tail, 119
liqueurs
 Amaro Averna liqueur, 81
 cherry liqueur, 124
 Grand Marnier liqueur, 53
 Maraschino liqueur, 15, 71, 79,
  102
 pear liqueur, 59
 specialty liqueurs, 15–16
 St-Germain liqueur, 79
London Dry Gin, 10
The Londoner. *See* Cucumber,
 Lemon & Dill Gin Infusion.
Love in Bloom, 52
Luxardo Maraschino liqueur
 Pear Blossom, 79
 Rhuby Daiquiri, 71

M

Mai Tai, 116
Man-Full-O'-Trouble Punch, 53
manual juicers, 23
Maraschino liqueur
    Hemingway Daiquiri, 102
    introduction, 15
    Pear Blossom, 79
    Rhuby Daiquiri, 71
Marshall, Barbie, 49, 50
martini glasses, 20
mason jars, 21
measuring cups, 24
measuring spoons, 24
Melon-choly Baby, 67
mescal
    agave nectar and, 27
    Bark and Blood, 62
    introduction, 12–13
mesh strainers, 17
Meskey, Maggie, 62
microplanes, 25
Mint Julep, 43
Mint Syrup, 40–43
Mixed Herb Syrup, 54–55
Mixtos Tequila, 12
Mojito, 41
Money Manhattan, 127
"Moonshine." *See* corn whiskey.
mugs, 21
Mumbai Mule, 59

N

Naughty Pilgrim, 59
"new generation" gins, 10–11
nonalcoholic beverages
    Blueberry Lemonade, 82
    Lavender Lemonade, 47
    Rosemary Lemonade, 44
None But the Brave, 119

O

O'Brien, Pat, 86
Ogden, Bradley, 138
Old-Fashioned glasses, 20
olive pitters, 25
Orange Bitters, 147
Orange-Cardamom Cooler, 68–69
Orange-Cardamom Syrup, 68–69
Orange Curaçao, 15
orange flower water, 31
Orgeat Syrup, 114–116
Oro Tequila, 12
oyster shooters, 135

P

paring knives, 17, 25
Parisian Martini, 46
Passion Fruit Syrup, 86–89
Peach Syrup, 43, 80–81
Pear Blossom, 79
pear liqueur, 59
Pear Syrup, 76–79
peelers, 17, 24
Peychaud, Antoine Amédée, 146
Pimento (or Allspice) Dram, 118–119
Piña Doble, 84–85
Pineapple Vodka Infusion, 132–133
Pink Sapphire Swizzle, 113
pitters, 25
Plata Tequila, 12
Plymouth Gin, 10
Polise, Maria, 117
pomegranate molasses, 31
port, 62
Port Light, 89
potato mashers, 25
power juicers, 23
produce, 29–30
proofs
    applejack, 96
    bitters, 146, 147, 150
    bourbon, 13
    Chartreuse, 16
    cognac, 15
    Ethanol, 130
    infusion bases, 130
    rum, 11
    Scotch whiskey, 14
    vodka, 10
Prosecco, 81
Provençal Martini, 48
Purple Haze, 100

R

Rabid Chihuahua, 139
Regan, Gary, 101, 138, 147
Reigel, Ryan, 120
reposado tequila
    Canción de Flores, 50
    introduction, 12
    Jalisco Cel-Ray, 74
    Piña Doble, 84–85
    Serafin, 138
    Tequila Por Mi Amante, 144
Rhubarb Syrup, 70–71
Rhuby Daiquiri, 71
rhum agricole
    Naughty Pilgrim, 59
    Rhuby Daiquiri, 71
    Rhum Ricardo, 117
"rocks" glasses, 20
rolling pins, 25
Rosalind Russell, 143
Rosemary Lemonade, 44

Rosemary Paloma, 45, 144
Rosemary Syrup, 44–45
Rose's Lime Juice Cordial, 101
rosewater, 31, 98, 106, 114
Royster Cup, 74
Ruby Red Grapefruit-Lemongrass Cordial, 102
rum
    as base for bitters, 150
    Basic Herbal Cooler, 55
    Basic Hot Toddy, 60
    Falernum, 117
    Hemingway Daiquiri, 102
    Hurricane, 86
    infusions, 129
    introduction, 11
    Mai Tai, 116
    Mojito, 41
    Pimento (or Allspice) Dram, 118–119
    Rhuby Daiquiri, 71
    Versailles, 120
Russell, Rosalind, 143
rye whiskey
    Basic Hot Toddy, 60
    Money Manhattan, 127
    Orange-Cardamom Cooler, 68–69
    Scofflaw, 97

S

salad spinners, 25
Salt of the Earth restaurant, 62
Salty Pomeranian, 107
Sandeman's Reserve port, 62
saucepans, 24
saucer glasses, 20
Saunders, Audrey, 112
Scofflaw, 97
Scotch whiskey
    Basic Hot Toddy, 60
    introduction, 14
Serafina Cocktail, 138
Serafin Infusion, 138
shakers, 17
Siegert, Alfredo, 146
Siegert, Carlos, 146
Siegert, Johann Gottlieb Benjamin, 146
silver tequila, 138
Simple Syrup
    Demerara Simple Syrup, 34, 117, 119, 142
    Falernum, 117
    Gin-Gin Mule, 112
    Homemade Aquavit, 142
    Homemade Limoncello, 140
    introduction, 33
    Lavender Lemonade, 47
    Lavender Syrup, 47

Lion's Tail, 119
Mint Syrup, 40
Mixed Herb Syrup, 54
None But the Brave, 119
Rabid Chihuahua, 139
recipe, 34–36
Rhuby Daiquiri, 71
Rosemary Lemonade, 44
Rosemary Syrup, 44
Salty Pomeranian, 107
Thai Basil Syrup, 38
Thyme Syrup, 46
single-grain Scotch whiskey, 14
single-malt Scotch whiskey, 14
Smoked Peach Bourbon Smash,
42, 149
Smoked Pineapple Syrup, 84–85
smokers, 25
Smokin' Mary, 121
sodas, 22
soda siphons, 23
Spice Bitters, 149
spice syrups
Cardamom-Kaffir Lime Syrup,
63–64
Cinnamon Syrup, 60–62
Dessert Spiced Syrup, 56, 59–60
Ginger Syrup, 66–67
introduction to spices, 28
Orange-Cardamom Syrup,
68–69
spoons, 17, 19, 24, 25
Steakhouse Pineapple Martini, 133
stevia, 27, 35
St-Germain liqueur, 79
stovetop smokers, 25
strainers, 17, 24
Strawberry Margarita, 145
sugars, 27, 34, 35
sweeteners, 27
syrups. See also cocktail starters.
blending, 36
Blueberry Syrup, 82
Celery Syrup, 73–74
Cinnamon Syrup, 60–62
Demerara Simple Syrup, 34,
117, 119, 142
Dessert Spiced Syrup, 56, 59–60
Falernum, 117
fruit/vegetable syrups, 70–91
Ginger Syrup, 66–67
herbal syrups, 37–55
Hibiscus Syrup, 51–53
Honeysuckle Syrup, 49–50
Lavender Syrup, 47–48
Mint Syrup, 40–43
Mixed Herb Syrup, 54–55
Orange-Cardamom Syrup,
68–69
Orgeat Syrup, 114–116

Passion Fruit Syrup, 86–89
Peach Syrup, 43, 80–81
Pear Syrup, 76–79
Rhubarb Syrup, 70–71
Rosemary Syrup, 44–45
Simple Syrup, 33, 34–36
Smoked Pineapple Syrup, 84–85
Spice Syrups, 56–69
storing, 35
Thai Basil Syrup, 38–39, 113
Thyme Syrup, 46
Truffle-Honey Syrup, 120
Turbinado Simple Syrup, 34, 35

T
tartaric acid powder, 31
tea cups, 21
tequila
agave nectar and, 27
Basic Herbal Cooler, 55
Canción de Flores, 50
Cardamom-Kaffir Lime Syrup,
63–64
introduction, 11–12
Jalisco Cel-Ray, 74
Orange-Cardamom Cooler,
68–69
Piña Doble, 84–85
Rosemary Paloma, 45, 144
Serafina Cocktail, 138
Serafin Infusion, 138
Strawberry Margarita, 145
Tequila Por Mi Amante, 144–145
Thai Basil Syrup, 38–39, 113
Thyme Syrup, 46
tools, 17–19, 24–26
Triple Sec, 15, 145
Truffle-Honey Syrup, 120
Turbinado Simple Syrup, 34, 35
turbinado sugar, 27

V
vegetable peelers, 17, 24
vermouth
Bark and Blood, 62
Gibson, 123
introduction, 15
Man-Full-O'-Trouble Punch, 53
Money Manhattan, 127
Scofflaw, 97
Versailles, 120
vodka
Basic Herbal Cooler, 55
Black Currant–Kaffir Lime
"Grenadine," 98
Bloody Viking, 143
Chihuahua Infusion, 139
Cold-Process Grenadine, 94
Cucumber Gimlet, 134

Cucumber Vodka Infusion,
133–134
Fresh Lemon Gimlet, 105
Fresh Lime Gimlet, 108
Grenadine, 94
Homemade Aquavit, 142–143
Homemade Limoncello,
140–141
Horseradish Vodka, 135
Hot Apple Pie, 61
introduction, 10
Limoncello, 140
Mumbai Mule, 59
Orange-Cardamom Cooler,
68–69
Orgeat Syrup, 114
Pear Blossom, 79
Pineapple Vodka Infusion,
132–133
Rabid Chihuahua, 139
Rosalind Russell, 143
Salty Pomeranian, 107
Simple Syrup, 34
Smokin' Mary, 121
Steakhouse Pineapple Martini,
133

W
whiskey. See bourbon; rye whiskey;
Scotch whiskey.
whisks, 25
Women Against Abuse, 64

Z
zesters, 17, 18, 25, 140

Don't miss these other titles from Quarry Books!

VINTAGE SPIRITS AND
FORGOTTEN COCKTAILS
978-1-59253-561-3

THE ART OF DISTILLING WHISKEY
AND OTHER SPIRITS
978-1-59253-569-9

EXTREME BREWING, A DELUXE
EDITION WITH 14 NEW
HOMEBREW RECIPES
978-1-59253-802-7

THE GOURMET'S GUIDE TO
COOKING WITH LIQUORS
AND SPIRITS
978-1-59253-594-1

THE BREWER'S APPRENTICE
978-1-59253-731-0

THE VINTNER'S APPRENTICE
978-1-59253-657-3

THE BACKYARD VINTNER
978-1-59253-198-1

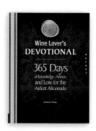

WINE LOVER'S DEVOTIONAL
978-1-59253-616-0

THE GOURMET'S GUIDE TO
COOKING WITH WINE
978-1-59253-470-8